PRAGMATISM AND IDEALISM

T0059397

Pragmatism and Idealism
Rorty and Hegel on Reason and Representation
Robert B. Brandom

The First Person in Cognition and Morality
Béatrice Longuenesse

PRAGMATISM AND IDEALISM

Rorty and Hegel on Reason and Representation

ROBERT B. BRANDOM

OXFORD
UNIVERSITY PRESS

OXFORD
UNIVERSITY PRESS

Great Clarendon Street, Oxford, OX2 6DP,
United Kingdom

Oxford University Press is a department of the University of Oxford.
It furthers the University's objective of excellence in research, scholarship,
and education by publishing worldwide. Oxford is a registered trade mark of
Oxford University Press in the UK and in certain other countries

First Edition published in 2022

Impression: 1

Published in the United States of America by Oxford University Press
198 Madison Avenue, New York, NY 10016, United States of America

British Library Cataloguing in Publication Data

Data available

Library of Congress Control Number: 2022940626

ISBN 978–0–19–287021–6

DOI: 10.1093/oso/9780192870216.001.0001

Printed and bound by
CPI Group (UK) Ltd, Croydon, CR0 4YY

CONTENTS

PREFACE

In early 2019, the University of Amsterdam philosophers invited me to take up the Spinoza Chair, and in connection with that post to deliver the Spinoza lectures there in the spring of 2020. I was privileged to be able to try out a first version of the material I was working on for those lectures at the second annual meeting of the Richard Rorty Society, at Penn State University in November 2019, at the invitation of Eduardo Mendieta. He and I were already working together on the project of publishing Rorty's 1996 Ferrater Mora lectures at the University of Girona (which appeared under Harvard University Press's distinguished Belknap imprint in 2021 with the title *Pragmatism as Anti-Authoritarianism*). Since those Girona lectures figured prominently in the story I wanted to tell, the Rorty Society was a natural venue that promised (and delivered) an interested and friendly audience. At that meeting I profited greatly from comments on the lectures by Rorty's lifelong friend and colleague, Richard Bernstein, and by Brady Bowman. The onset of the Covid-19 pandemic required that my visit to Amsterdam be postponed until 2021—and in the end, both my seminar and all my lectures, including the Spinoza lectures, ended up having to be delivered remotely for the same reason. I am very sorry to have missed the opportunity to spend a semester at the University of Amsterdam in person. I would like to thank my gracious hosts there, especially Professor Beate Roessler, who overcame the disruptions to make the whole interaction pleasant, stimulating, and constructive, in spite of the difficult circumstances.

Lecture 1

PRAGMATISM AS COMPLETING THE ENLIGHTENMENT

Reason against Representation

I

Generations of German philosophy students were taught early on that they face a stark, ineluctable, existentially defining choice: "Kant, oder Hegel?" The thought was not that one needed to pick one or the other of these seminal, difficult, multifarious philosophers to concentrate on and master. It was that, struggle as one might, one would inevitably find oneself *allied* with one or the other—conceptually, methodologically, and even temperamentally—and that the difference would resonate throughout one's thought, beyond one's conscious control, affecting the topics one found it important to address, the tools one used to do so, the manner in which one proceeded, and the standards to which one held oneself. If they got a bit further, the students would learn to line this question up with the more focused one: "*Verstand oder Vernunft?*" This is asking whether one organizes one's thought and philosophical

Pragmatism and Idealism: Rorty and Hegel on Reason and Representation. Robert B. Brandom, Oxford University Press. © Robert B. Brandom 2022. DOI: 10.1093/oso/9780192870216.003.0001

aspirations according to the metacategories of scientific *under-standing* or of the more exalted and self-reflective *reason*, in something like the sense Hegel gave to this originally Kantian distinction. If the students didn't get that far, the question would still live on for them in the form of a vague background concern with how seriously to take the Romantics' critique of the Enlightenment.

Though he himself never put the point like this, I think a useful way to understand the basic principle animating the two books in which Richard Rorty first found his distinctive philosophical voice—*Philosophy and the Mirror of Nature* (1979) and *Consequences of Pragmatism* (1982)—is as applying a sophisticated form of this "Kant oder Hegel?" framework to then contemporary analytic philosophy. So construed, the critique and diagnosis of the ills of the kind of philosophy he found himself immersed in at Princeton that is developed at length in *Mirror* condemn it for its Kantianism. (When at the end of that book, in a phrase he came not only to reject, but to regret, he prophesied the "death of philosophy," the quintessential anti-essentialist explicitly defined what he meant by the term "philosophy"— what he thought we could, and urged we should, no longer go on doing—as "the sort of thing that Kant did.") And the new kind of pragmatism with which Rorty proposed to replace that sort of philosophy is evidently and avowedly Hegelian in spirit—albeit inspired by the naturalized (but still social and historical) form of Hegelianism he admired in Dewey and self-consciously emulated in his own work.

Later, Rorty would applaud the broadly naturalistic, sociological, historicist impulse he saw Hegel as having bequeathed to the nascent nineteenth century, and speculate about how much further we might have gotten by now if at the end of that century Russell and Husserl had not, each in his own way, once again found something for philosophers to be apodeictic about, from their armchairs. Rorty's idea of the form of a justification for a recommendation of a way forward always was a redescription of *where we have gotten to*, motivated by a Whiggish story about *how we got here* that clearly marks off both the perils already encountered and the progress already achieved along that path. This is the literary genre of which Rorty is an undisputed master. He said that already during his undergraduate years at the University of Chicago:

> Hegel's *Phenomenology of Spirit*, Whitehead's *Adventures of Ideas*, and Lovejoy's *The Great Chain Being* gave me a taste for ambitious, swooshy, *Geistesgeschichte* that I have never lost. This taste was gratified in later years by such writers as Étienne Gilson, Hans Blumenberg, and, above all, the later Heidegger. My taste for synoptic narratives has sometimes made me think that my real *métier* was intellectual history, and that I might have been better off in that discipline than in philosophy.[1]

Rorty here explicitly acknowledges his appreciation of the literary genre that Hegel both brilliantly practiced and centrally thematized, putting Hegel's distinctive new master metaconcept of *recollective rationality* at the center of his own approach.

It might seem that bringing the Kant versus Hegel conceptual framework to bear to illuminate the state of Anglophone philosophy in the last third of the twentieth century was no great innovation and required no great insight. After all, hadn't that tradition already pugnaciously divided itself into analytic and continental camps that more or less lined up with that

---

[1] Pp. 5–6 of Rorty's "Intellectual Autobiography" in the Schilpp volume *The Philosophy of Richard Rorty* in the Library of Living Philosophers series (Vol. 32), edited by Randall E. Auxier and Lewis Edwin Hahn (Chicago, IL: Open Court Publishing, 2007).

framework—with a more narrowly professionalized research discipline using technical definitions and formalized arguments to address problems construed as perennial, and an epistemological focus on empirical science, on the one side, and on the other side a more broadly intellectual, thoroughly historicized, self-consciously hermeneutic pursuit, more interested in literature, art, and politics? But further reflection undercuts simply lining up these movements with Kant and Hegel. It is true that it was the continentalists, and not the analysts, who continued to read Hegel. But among the towering figures in that tradition, Husserl decisively identified himself with Kant rather than Hegel, and Heidegger had quite complicated attitudes toward both figures, unified in the end by his violent recoil from and vehement rejection of the pair of them, and all they stood for ("the horse they rode in on"). In any case, the broadly Hegelian project Rorty was then recommending as an alternative to the degenerating Kantian research program he saw in analytic philosophy did not look to Europe for its inspiration, but to the substantially distinct tradition of classical American pragmatism.

Rorty's remarkable diagnosis of the ills of analytic philosophy as resulting from an uncritical, so undigested, Kantianism is at least equally radical and surprising as the reimagined, redescribed, and revived pragmatism that he developed as a constructive therapeutic response to it. For Kant emphatically was *not* a hallowed hero of that tradition. Anglophone analytic philosophers thought that the "Kant oder Hegel?" question simply didn't apply to them. After all, Russell and Moore had read Kant out of the analytic canon alongside Hegel—believing (I think, correctly as it has turned out) that one couldn't open the door wide enough to let Kant into the canon without Hegel sliding in alongside him before that door could be slammed shut. Both figures were banished, paraded out of town under a banner of shame labeled "idealism," whose canonical horrible paradigm was the Bradleyan British Idealism of the Absolute, from which those codifiers of the analytic paradigm were recoiling—having been acolytes early on. So in diagnosing twentieth-century analytic philosophy as constrained by conceptual bounds put on it by Kant, Rorty in *Philosophy and the Mirror of Nature* was in fact taking a remarkable and original line: offering a retrospective redescription and reconceptualization that was both disquieting and disorienting. The dominant self-conception (combatively made explicit by Carnap) was of analytic philosophy as an up-to-date form of *empiricism*, a specifically *logical* empiricism, whose improvement on traditional, pre-Kantian, Early Modern British empiricism consisted in the much more sophisticated sort of logical tools it deployed to structure and bind together essentially the same atoms of pre-conceptual sensory experience to which the earlier empiricists had appealed.

II

To see why and how Rorty blamed Kant for what he saw as the calamitous state and degenerating research program of analytic philosophy in the second half of the twentieth century, one must look more closely at the argument of *Philosophy and the Mirror of Nature*. Its most focused target is epistemological foundationalism. Rorty saw epistemology as unable to escape the Agrippan trilemma. Attempts to justify empirical knowledge must either move in a circle, embark on an infinite regress, or end by appeal to unjustified justifiers, which must accordingly supply the foundations on which all cognition rests. The animating thought is that justifying, by inferring conclusions from premises, can only *transmit* antecedently possessed positive justificatory status. So the first two options lead to skepticism about justification.

On the third, foundationalist, option, two kinds of justificatory regress threaten. For when a set of premises is appealed to in justifying a conclusion, one can inquire further after the warrant either of those *premises*, or of the *implication* of the conclusion *by* the premises. The two sorts of regress-stoppers Rorty saw appealed to by epistemological foundationalists were immediate sensory experiences, as ultimate justifiers of *premises*, and immediate grasp of the meanings of our terms or the contents of our concepts, as ultimate justifiers of *inferences*. In a telling phrase, he refers to these as two sorts of "epistemically privileged representations." (The phrase is revelatory because and insofar as *privilege* is a *normative* concept, and as we shall see, it is that kind of concept that his later social pragmatism principally addresses.)

Rorty takes Kant at his word when Kant says that what he is doing is synthesizing rationalism and empiricism. But Rorty takes it that what logical empiricism made of Kant's synthesis in the end takes over *both* sorts of privileged representations: the sensory given from the empiricists, and the rational (logical, inferential, semantic) given from the rationalists. This is one sense in which Rorty diagnoses Anglophone philosophy as still in thrall to Kantian commitments. In this story, Carnap shows up as a neo-Kantian *malgré lui*—though that is not at all how he thought of or presented himself. It is, however, how Rorty's hero Wilfrid Sellars regarded Carnap. (Perhaps the revenant neo-Kantian philosophical spirit of Heinrich Rickert, passed on through his student Bruno Bauch, Frege's friend and colleague and Carnap's *Doktorvater*, was just too strong to be wholly exorcised by the empiricist rites and rituals practiced by the Vienna Circle.) But the roots of these foundationalist commitments can be traced back even further, to Descartes. For he assimilated the images delivered by the senses and the thoughts arising in intellect together under the umbrella concept of *pensées* precisely in virtue of what he saw as their shared epistemic transparency and incorrigibility. These were precisely the features needed for them to perform the regress-stopping function in a foundationalist epistemological response to the skeptical threat posed by the other two alternatives in the traditional trilemma.

In rejecting both sensory givenness and meaning- or concept-analytic inferential connections, Rorty relies on the arguments of two of Carnap's most important and insightful admirers and critics: Sellars in "Empiricism and the Philosophy of Mind" and Quine in "Two Dogmas of Empiricism," respectively.[2] (These are in any case surely two of the most important philosophical essays of the 1950s.) Tellingly, and with characteristic insight, Rorty finds a common root in their apparently quite different critiques. Sellars and Quine, he sees, both offer ultimately *pragmatist* arguments, which find the *theoretical* postulation of such privileged representations to be unable to explain cardinal features of the *practices* of applying empirical concepts.

Rorty then widens the focus of his own critique by deepening the diagnosis that animates it. The original source of *foundationalism* in *epistemology*, he claims, is *representationalism* in *semantics*. Thinking of the mind in terms of *representation* was Descartes's invention. But the idea was brought to a new level of sophistication by Kant. He codified representation as the semantic genus

---

[2] These particular arguments are assembled for this anti-foundationalist purpose with exceptional clarity in Rorty's student Michael Williams's dissertation, rewritten as *Groundless Belief* (New Haven, CT: Yale University Press, 1977).

of which both sensory intuitions and inference-engendering concepts are species, and certified our epistemological privileged access to both under the residually Cartesian slogan "Nothing is better known to the mind than itself." It is perhaps ironic that in digging down beneath epistemological issues to unearth the semantic presuppositions that shape and enable them, Rorty is following Kant's example. For Kant's argument, culminating in the "Refutation of Idealism," was that once we understood how to respond to the threat of *semantic* skepticism about the intelligibility of the relation between representings and what they represent, there would be left no residual issue concerning *epistemological* skepticism about whether any such relations actually obtained: whether things were ever as we represent them to be.

In the end, I think that while Rorty's objections to foundationalism are made pretty clear in the text, the rationale for laying responsibility for this epistemological view on semantic appeal to the concept of *representation* are less so. But putting together clues he offers us, an argument for seeing the necessity for two sorts of objectionably privileged representations as already implicit in the idea that the mind's cognitive relation to its world is representational might be reconstructed along the following lines. The starting point is the Cartesian idea that if we are to understand ourselves as knowing the world by representing it (so that error is to be understood as *mis*representation), there must be *some* kind of thing that we can know *non*-representationally—namely, our representings themselves. On pain of an infinite regress, knowledge of representeds mediated by representings of them must involve immediate (that is, non-representational) knowledge of at least *some* representings. Our nonrepresentational relation to these representings will be epistemically privileged, in the sense of being immune to error. For error is construed exclusively as misrepresentation. (This is the representationalist semantic analogue of the justificatory epistemological regress on the side of premises.)

Next is the thought that when we ask about our knowledge of the *relation* between representings and representeds, another potential regress looms if we are obliged to think of *this* knowledge also in representational terms, that is, as mediated by representings of it. (This is the representationalist semantic analogue of the justificatory epistemological regress on the side of inferences.) On this dimension, too, appeal to immediate, nonrepresentational access to representational relations seems necessary. The pair of threatened semantic regresses, one on the side of relations and the other on the side of their relata, exactly parallels the pair of threatened epistemological regresses invoked by the Agrippan trilemma. Along both dimensions, the threat of an infinite regress seems to force a choice between foundationalism and skepticism, depending on whether we invoke something known immediately and nonrepresentationally, or allow that mediation by representings goes all the way down. Rorty saw that according to such a picture, the *epistemological* choice between foundationalism and skepticism is already built deeply into the structure of the *semantic* representational model.

III

Looking back, in his intellectual autobiography, Rorty said:

> I still believe most of what I wrote in *Philosophy and the Mirror of Nature*. But that book is now out of date.... I vaguely sensed that the trouble with analytic philosophy was that it had never advanced from Kant's eternalization of the intellectual situation of eighteenth-century Europe to Hegel's historicism. But I had

not yet made myself sufficiently familiar with the post-Hegelian European philosophers who had resisted the temptation to go "back to Kant."[3]

I think Rorty came to be dissatisfied with the *Philosophy and the Mirror of Nature* strategy of arguing against representationalist paradigms in semantics on the basis that they force an epistemological choice between skepticism and foundationalism. He never wavered in his view that finding oneself in that epistemological predicament demonstrates the need for radical conceptual revision of one's semantic model. And he continued to believe that the concept of *representation* was so burdened by epistemological baggage that a new start was needed. But his strategy for delegitimizing representational semantic models changed. He realized that as a matter of sociological fact, concern with epistemological skepticism and foundationalism were not in fact central, orienting concerns of the analytic philosophy of his day, centered as it was on the philosophy of language. He still identified the ultimate culprit and enemy as semantic representationalism. And he saw that it was still the orienting and organizing principle of philosophy of language and philosophy of mind. (His Princeton colleague David Lewis had already been busily developing and reinforcing the edifice of possible world semantics for some time when Rorty wrote *Mirror*.) Yet those who took representational models of semantics for granted were for the most part blithely unconcerned with the supposedly life-and-death struggle between skepticism and foundationalism. During the last decade of his life Rorty formulated a new line of attack: seeing anti-representationalism in semantics as a version of pragmatist anti-*authoritarianism*. This more overtly

[3] Rorty, "Intellectual Autobiography," p. 13.

political line both drew on and, in an important sense, brought to a logical conclusion the evolution of his thought in the intervening decades. This is the argument and the development I want to consider in more detail.

He introduced the new idea in his June 1996 Ferrater Mora lectures at the University of Girona, entitled "Anti-Authoritarianism in Epistemology and Ethics."[4] In connection with those lectures, he was encouraged to invite discussants of his choice. I was privileged to be among them, along with my colleague John McDowell, and Bjorn Ramberg, whose sympathetic yet penetrating reading of Davidson had deeply impressed Rorty. One memorable extended discussion during those happy days led to a consensus among us about how three of our positions should be understood in relation to one another. We all agreed that if one found oneself obliged to choose between epistemological skepticism and epistemological foundationalism, then somewhere well upstream something had gone badly wrong conceptually. Shifting the metaphor, that predicament could be thought of as a bottomless abyss that must be avoided at all costs.

Rorty's view was that one put oneself severely at peril of falling into that chasm as soon as one permitted oneself to think in terms of the concepts of *experience* and *representation* at all. Although he conceded that these powerful and

---

[4] Published as *El pragmatismo, una version: Antiautoristarismo en epistemologia y ética*, trans. Joan Verges Gifra (Barcelona: Ariel, 2000). These lectures were not published in English during his lifetime. The English text is included in the Richard Rorty Papers among the Special Collections and Archives at the University of California, Irvine Libraries ("Born digital writings"—Subseries 8.7, 1988–2003). The lectures have now been published in full in English in a volume edited and with an Afterword by Eduardo Mendieta, with Rorty's own Preface, and a Foreword by me under the title *Pragmatism as Anti-Authoritarianism* (Cambridge, MA: Harvard University Press, 2021).

dangerous philosophical concepts—one epistemological, the other semantic—were progressively and productively employed beginning in Early Modern times, he took it that we were now in a position to see where their use inevitably led: free-fall into the abyss, doomed to oscillate endlessly between skepticism and foundationalism. To keep us safe, Rorty thought, a protective fence needs to be erected sufficiently far from the edge that the temptation of the dilemma would not even be visible from the safe side of that fence. His radical proposal then, as already in *Philosophy and the Mirror of Nature*, was that both concepts must be given up once and for all. For Rorty, a principal virtue of the sort of pragmatism he endorsed and developed as a successor framework is that it had no need and no use for the traditional concepts of *experience* and *representation* in talking about how vocabularies help us cope with the vicissitudes of life. Indeed, from a pragmatist point of view, the very distinction between epistemology and semantics becomes unnecessary—a lesson he took himself to have learned from "Two Dogmas." As he thought of it, pragmatism carves out an entirely different conceptual path from the modern philosophical tradition that grew up around those concepts. He sums up his anti-representationalist linguistic pragmatism in the pithy slogan: "language is for *coping*, not *copying*." He also used to repeat with approval Rebecca West's irritated rejection of mimetic approaches to art, as paraphrased by Nelson Goodman: "A copy of the universe is not what is required. One of the damned things is enough."

Rorty thought that if it were possible for the concept of *experience* to be rehabilitated, if it *could* be purged of its Cartesian contagion, then surely Dewey would have been the one to have brought it off. Dewey worked tirelessly to give "experience" the processual, interactive, broadly ecological sense of Hegelian "Erfahrung," rather than the atomic, episodic, self-intimating, epistemically transparent Cartesian sense of "Erlebnis." (Dewey's is the sense in which, as he says, it is perfectly in order for a job advertisement to specify "No experience necessary." It is not intended to be read in the Cartesian sense, which would invite applications from zombies.) But Dewey signally failed to get the philosophical and generally cultured public to shake off the Cartesian associations of the term. And his own practice degenerated to the point that, as Rorty said (thinking especially of Dewey's practice in *Experience and Nature*), "he ended up using the term 'experience' merely as an incantatory device to blur every conceivable distinction." Rorty remained convinced that Dewey had been right to eschew representation talk as giving aid and comfort to exactly the sort of static, spectatorial, intellectualist, "mind as the mirror of nature" views that lead to the skepticism/foundationalism dilemma. Ramberg agreed with Rorty on these basic points.

I was entirely of his mind as far as the concept of *experience* is concerned. Outside of explicitly Hegelian contexts, where it figures in his conception of recollective rationality, it is not one of my words. It is not used (but only mentioned) in the many pages of *Making It Explicit*, even where topics such as perceptual knowledge are addressed. I agree that the associations and correlated inferential temptations entrained with the term "experience" go too deep, easily to be jettisoned, or even for us to succeed in habituating ourselves completely to resist.[5] The light of day neither drives out the shadows nor stays the

[5] A bold and powerful, conceptually revisionary stratagem that gives me pause in this assessment is due to Anil Gupta's recent work—see his *Conscious Experience* (Cambridge, MA: Harvard University Press, 2019). He shows us how to think of experience as a nonconceptual force that is articulated by the transformations of conceptual commitments it occasions.

night. We are on the whole better off training ourselves to do without this notion.

But by contrast to the concept of *experience*, it seemed to me then, and seems to me still, that things are otherwise with the concept of *representation*. There are many things one might mean by "anti-representationalism." When I use the term "representationalism," I mean a particular order of semantic explanation. It starts with a notion of *representational content* (reference, extension, or truth conditions) and understands proprieties of *inference* in terms of such already representationally contentful contents. Those contents must accordingly be assumed to be, or made to be, theoretically and explanatorily intelligible antecedently to and independently of the role of representations in inference. "Representationalism" in this sense contrasts with *inferentialist* orders of semantic explanation, which begin with a notion of content understood in terms of role in reasoning, and proceed from there to explain the representational dimension of discursive content. I recommend and pursue inferentialist rather than representationalist semantic explanations.

But not giving *representation* a fundamental explanatory role in semantics does not disqualify it from playing any role whatsoever. And subsequent discussions with Huw Price (another younger pragmatist after the linguistic turn for whose work Rorty expressed particular enthusiasm) have made clear that there is a big difference between *rejecting global representationalism*, in the sense of denying that the best semantics for *all* kinds of expressions assigns them a fundamentally representational role, and being a *global anti-representationalist*, by insisting that *no* expressions should be understood semantically to play representational roles.[6] Perhaps their representational roles are

---

[6] I discuss this issue further in "Global Anti-Representationalism?" In *Expressivism, Pragmatism, and Representationalism* Huw Price, Simon Blackburn,

essential to the content and use of some kinds of expressions (such as ordinary empirical descriptive locutions) and not to others (such as logical, modal, or normative locutions). It seemed to me in Girona, and still does today, that a suitable pragmatist explanatory strategy, beginning with social practices of using expressions to give and ask for reasons, could unobjectionably both underwrite theoretical attributions of representational content to some locutions and also underwrite the viability and utility of the common-sense distinction between what we are saying or thinking and what we are talking or thinking *about*—that is, representing or describing *by* saying or thinking that. In particular, I pointed then to the *Making It Explicit* strategy for explaining what one is *doing* in using the principal representational locutions of ordinary language—*de re* ascriptions of propositional attitudes, such as "Benjamin Franklin believed *of electrons* that they flowed through metal and not glass,"—as expressing explicitly differences of *social* perspective among various interlocutors.

So it seemed to me that a distinction should be made between the reprobate, irremediably tainted concept of *experience*, which should be banished from careful philosophical discourse, and the prodigal, errant, and admittedly potentially dangerous concept of *representation*, which might still be tamed, rehabilitated, sanitized, and reintroduced to perform carefully supervised productive labor in a new, hygienic guise. In the image we all found useful, I thought the fence keeping us from sliding into the abyss of the foundationalism-or-skepticism epistemological dilemma could be located *much* closer to the edge than Rorty did.

Although, by contrast to the notion of *experience*, the concept of *representation* is not a particular focus of McDowell's *Mind and*

Robert Brandom, Paul Horwich, and Michael Williams (Cambridge: Cambridge University Press, 2013).

World, he was, and is, convinced that *both* concepts can be relieved of the excess baggage of associations that, he agrees, *can* and *have* made them principal villains enticing philosophers to their doom down the path that leads to the foundationalism-or-skepticism oscillation Rorty convincingly diagnoses. Rorty and I agreed that McDowell had successfully brought off the feat of disciplining a notion of *experience* to the point where it could do crucial philosophical work without falling into Sellars's Myth of the Given. Given that remarkable achievement, it is no surprise that the relaxed way in which he invokes the representational dimension of empirical concept use also manages not to be philosophically theory-laden in a way that leads to the troubles Rorty diagnoses. It helps here that McDowell shares with Rorty a Wittgensteinian version of the pragmatist anti-metaphysical conviction. That conviction entails that calling on *any* concept to do heavy lifting in philosophical explanations of some supposedly puzzling phenomenon (such as the possibility of genuinely knowing how things visibly are) is infallibly a sign of deep antecedent conceptual confusion in understanding the situation that seems to call for that distinctive philosophical kind of explanation.

As a result of his resolute rejection of the impulse for deep metaphysical explanation, McDowell doesn't think that a fence is necessary to avoid the abyss at all. If we are just sufficiently careful with our use of the concepts of *experience* and *representation*, cutting them free of entanglement with dubious and ultimately disreputable metaphysical, epistemological, and semantic programs motivated by ill-posed and ill-considered questions, we can keep carefully circumscribed versions of the ordinary language terms around and use them as necessary in philosophical clarifications. He shows that *is* possible by skipping merrily along the very edge of the foundationalist precipice, sure-footed as a mountain goat, never putting a foot wrong or seeming to be in danger of losing his balance.

Rorty and I agree that McDowell brings this off. But we want to say "Kids, don't try this at home. This man is a skilled professional. It is not as easy as it looks." The balancing act can indeed be brought off, because he can do it and does do it. We thought that prudence nonetheless dictates the erection of a fence to protect the unwary, less careful, and less skilled philosophical public from what remains a dangerous temptation. McDowell seemed to us not to be sufficiently concerned about the danger to those less capable than himself. Edinburgh stringently enforces a legal prohibition on jaywalking (crossing the street against the traffic signals)—which is illegal if and only if it is done within sight of anyone under the age of twelve. The motivating principle being enforced is: risk your own life, but don't encourage the young and impressionable to follow suit and risk theirs. McDowell, we felt, insufficiently appreciates the practical wisdom of the Edinburgh rules when applied to the metaphilosophical case.

IV

This three-sided discussion in Girona was in many ways a satisfying survey for us all. It usefully rehearsed and fixed our general locations in philosophical space, along with the hopes and suspicions that motivated them. At the end of it, Rorty told us that what we would hear about in his immediately upcoming lectures was a new line of argument against representationalism. It took the form of a recharacterization of the lesson and significance of the pragmatism that he had all along aimed to establish as the principal rival of, and ultimate successor to, the pervasive representationalism of the day. According to this new way of pitching things, what pragmatism aims at—beginning already, if only incipiently, with the classical American pragmatists—is nothing less than a second Enlightenment.

My principal concern here is with the particular way Rorty picks up and develops a line of thought he identifies in Dewey, elaborating it into a distinctive, anti-fetishist, anti-authoritarian version of a specifically pragmatist second Enlightenment—or, sometimes, as the second phase needed to complete the original one. Before laying out the new Enlightenment vision that Rorty articulates in his Girona lectures at the end of the twentieth century, however, I want to fill in some of the background picture of how the classical American pragmatism that took shape a hundred years earlier could credibly be seen as already enacting a second Enlightenment. This is a picture I think Rorty largely takes for granted, but never specifically expounds in the terms I will suggest. Rehearsing it provides important context for Rorty's move, and, I think, both strengthens his case and serves to highlight his further contribution to the tradition he both inherits from his American pragmatist heroes and retrospectively rationally reconstructs. The story I will outline is a broad, but I hope recognizable, characterization of the constellation of ideas that Peirce bequeaths to James and Dewey, and through them, to Rorty.[7]

The motor of the first Enlightenment was the rise of the new natural science—in particular, the mathematized physics of Galileo, Descartes, and Newton. The philosophical project

---

[7] I tell the story retailed here in somewhat more detail in the context of an extended review of Louis Menand's wonderful book *The Metaphysical Club* in "When Philosophy Paints Its Blue on Grey: Irony and the Pragmatist Enlightenment," *boundary* 2, Vol. 29, No. 2, Summer 2002, pp. 1–28.

animated by its spectacular achievements centered on the question: what should the fact that these new empirical and theoretical practices turn out to be the best way to understand the nonhuman world teach us about the nature of that world, about what knowledge and understanding are, and about ourselves as knowers in that sense of, and agents in, the world as science reveals it to be? Because their thought was principally oriented by this project, all of the canonical philosophers from Descartes through Kant can sensibly be understood as at base philosophers of science.

The physical science they were inspired by and interpreters of put forward mathematical theories in the form of impersonal, immutable principles formulating universal, eternal, necessary laws. Enlightenment empiricism sought to ground all our knowledge in self-contained, self-intimating sensory episodes whose brute occurrence is the most basic kind of knowing. Just how the natural light of reason could extract secure and certain knowledge of things as law-governed from those deliverances of fallible perception was a perennial puzzle. A further problem was fitting into the picture of the world as delivered by the best science of the time the sensing, theorizing, and experimentally intervening scientific minds with which we were encouraged to identify ourselves. Even had Hume succeeded in his aspiration to become "the Newton of the mind" by perfecting Locke's theoretical efforts to understand the psychological processes of understanding in terms of mechanisms of association and abstraction, the issue of how the subject of that science was to be found among the furniture of the universe described by the real Newton would have survived untouched, as an apparently intractable philosophical embarrassment.

The founding genius of American pragmatism, Charles Sanders Peirce, was, like the original Enlightenment *philosophes,* above all, a philosopher of science. He, too, took as his basic philosophical project the task of explaining what the best science of his time taught us ontologically about the ultimate nature of the world we live in, epistemologically about the character of the best understanding of it as epitomized by that science, and about how we should understand that world as (in Jay Rosenberg's phrase) "growing knowers." But the contemporary sciences that provided his master ideas were very different from those that set the agenda for seventeenth- and eighteenth-century philosophers. He was impressed by the broadly *selectional* forms of explanation that he presciently saw as common to Darwinian evolutionary biology, at the level of species, and the latest psychological theories of learning, at the level of individual organisms. And he was also impressed by the new forms of *statistical* explanation that were both essential to the new physical science of thermodynamics and becoming increasingly central to the new social sciences of the late nineteenth century.

A principal feature distinguishing both selectional and statistical forms of explanation from the Newtonian model of explaining particular occurrences by deriving them from or subsuming them under universal laws is that instead of showing how what actually happened *had* to happen—why what is actual is at least conditionally *necessary*—the new methodologies make it possible to explain events that are acknowledged to be contingent and merely *probable*. Accounts that appeal to natural selection in biology, or to supervised selection in learning, or to statistical likelihood (whether in physics or sociology or economics), show how observed order can arise, contingently, but explicably, out of an irregular background of variation—as the cumulative result of individually random, contingent happenings. Peirce saw this as nothing less than a new form of intelligibility. Understanding whose paradigm is Darwin's evolutionary theory is a concrete, situated narrative of local, contingent, mutable, practical, reciprocal accommodations of particular creatures and habitats. Peirce speculatively generalized this model to a vision in which even the most fundamental laws of physics are understood as contingently emerging by selectional processes from primordial indeterminateness. No less than the behavior of biological organisms, those laws are to be understood as *adaptational habits*, each of which is in a statistical sense relatively stable and robust in the environment provided by the rest. The old forms of scientific explanation then appear as special, limiting cases of the new. The now restricted validity of appeal to laws and universal principles is explicable against the wider background provided by the new scientific paradigms of how regularity can arise out of and be sustained by variability. The "calm realm of laws" of the first Enlightenment becomes for the second a dynamic population of habits, winnowed from a larger one, which has so far escaped extinction by maintaining a more or less fragile collective self-reproductive equilibrium.

Since laws emerge only statistically, they may change. No Darwinian adaptation is final, for the environment it is adapting to might change—indeed must eventually change, in response to other Darwinian adaptations. And the relatively settled, fixed properties of things, their *habits*, as Peirce and Dewey would say, are themselves to be understood just as such adaptations. Peirce was a naturalist, but through the lens of then contemporary science he confronted a new sort of nature, a nature that is fluid, stochastic, with regularities being the statistical products of many particular contingent interactions between things and their ever changing environments, hence emergent and potentially evanescent, floating statistically on a sea of chaos.

Like many of the philosophers of the original Enlightenment, Peirce combined ontological naturalism (of his new, statistical-selectional kind) with epistemological empiricism. Like them, too, Peirce and his pragmatist followers subscribed to Wilfrid Sellars's *scientia mensura* doctrine: "In the dimension of describing and explaining, science is the measure of all things: of those that are, that they are, and of those that are not that they are not."[8] And for both groups, science is not just *one* sort, but the very form of knowing: what it knows not, is not knowledge. But just as Peirce's was a naturalism based on a radically different conception of nature, so his empiricism was based on a radically different conception of experience. The science to which the later pragmatist Enlightenment looked for its inspiration had changed since that of the earlier in more than just the conceptual resources and the distinctive new forms of scientific intelligibility that it offered to its philosophical interpreters and admirers.

In the seventeenth and eighteenth centuries, the impact of science was still largely a matter of its *theories*. Its devotees dreamed of, predicted, and planned for great social and political transformations that they saw the insights of the new science as prefiguring and preparing. But during this period those new ways of thinking centered around the Scientific Revolution were largely devoid of immediate practical consequences. By the middle of the nineteenth century, though, technology, the practical arm of science, had changed the world radically and irrevocably through the Industrial Revolution. From the vantage point of established industrial capitalism, science appeared as the most spectacularly successful social institution of the previous 200 years because it had become not only a *practice*,

---

[8] Wilfrid Sellars, *Empiricism and the Philosophy of Mind* (Cambridge, MA: Harvard University Press, 1998), section 63.

but a *business.* Its practical successes paraded as the warrant of its claims to theoretical insight. Technology *embodies* understanding. The more general philosophical lessons the pragmatists drew from science for an understanding of the nature of reason and its central role in human life accordingly sought to comprehend intellectual understanding as an aspect of effective agency, to situate knowing *that* (some claim is true) in the larger field of knowing *how* (to do something). The sort of explicit reason that can be codified in principles appears as just one, often dispensable, expression of the sort of implicit intelligence that can be exhibited in skillful, because experienced, practice—flexible, adaptable habit that has emerged in a particular environment, by selection via a learning process.

Thinking of scientific practices primarily from the side of technology rather than theory is the key to the pragmatists' updated form of empiricism. For them the unit of experience is a Test-Operate-Test-Exit cycle of perception, action, and further perception of the results of the action. On this model, experience is not an *input* to the process of learning. Experience *is* the process of learning: the statistical emergence by selection of behavioral variants that survive and become habits insofar as they are, in company with their fellows, adaptive in the environments in which they are successively and successfully exercised. The rationality of science is best epitomized not in the occasion of the theorist's sudden intellectual glimpse of some aspect of the true structure of reality, but in the process by which the skilled practitioner coaxes usable observations by experimental intervention, crafts theories by inferential postulation and extrapolation, and dynamically works out a more or less stable but always evolving accommodation between the provisional results of those two enterprises. The distinctive pragmatist shift in imagery for the mind is not from mirror to lamp, but from telescope and microscope to flywheel governor.

These new forms of naturalism and empiricism, updated so as to be responsive to the changed character and circumstances of nineteenth-century science, meshed with each other far better than their predecessors had. Early Modern philosophers notoriously had trouble fitting human knowledge and agency into its mechanist, materialist version of the natural world. A Cartesian chasm opened up between the activity of the theorist whose understanding consists in the manipulation of algebraic symbolic representings, and what is thereby understood: the extended, geometrical world represented by those symbols. This was precisely the gap that the concept of *representation* was designed to fill. Its difficulties in doing so are what raise the specter of skepticism. The difficulty for philosophers of the first Enlightenment was that understanding, discovering, and acting on principles exhibited for them one sort of intelligibility, with matter moving according to eternal, ineluctable, mathematically expressible laws another. On the pragmatist understanding, however, knower and known are alike explicable by appeal to the same general mechanisms that bring order out of chaos, settled habit from random variation: the statistical selective structure shared by processes of evolution and of learning. That selectional structure ties together all the members of a great continuum of being stretching from the processes by which physical regularities emerge, through those by which the organic evolves locally and temporarily stable forms, through the learning processes by which the animate acquire locally and temporarily adaptive habits, to the intelligence of the untutored common sense of ordinary language users, and ultimately to the methodology of the scientific theorist—which is just the explicit, systematic refinement of the implicit, unsystematic but nonetheless intelligent procedures character-istic of everyday practical life. For the first time, the rational practices embodying the paradigmatic sort of reason exercised by scientists understanding natural processes become visible as continuous with, and intelligible in just the same terms as, the physical processes paradigmatic of what is understood. This unified vision stands at the center of the classical American pragmatists' second Enlightenment.

This happy concord and consilience between the distinctively pragmatist versions of naturalism in ontology and empiricism in epistemology stands in stark contrast, not only to the prior traditional British empiricism of the Enlightenment, but also to the subsequent twentieth-century logical empiricism of the Vienna Circle. The reductive physicalist version of naturalism and the reductive phenomenalist version of empiricism they inclined to endorse were exceptionally difficult to reconcile with each other. Hume had already shown how difficult it is to provide suitable empiricist credentials for the way in which mathematical laws supporting subjunctive reasoning—the crowning glory of Newtonian physics—outrun observable reg-ularities, not only epistemically, but semantically. Adding the powerful methods of modern logic to articulate the phenomenal deliverances of sense did not alter this fundamental mismatch. A threatening and recalcitrant tension accordingly concerned how to proceed when respect for the deliverances of natural science as the measure of what there is and how it is in nature collides with empiricist strictures on when we are entitled to claim to know what there is and how it is. Otto Neurath thought that naturalism should prevail, while Moritz Schlick thought that empiricism should. Rudolf Carnap struggled mightily to keep these two wings of the movement from flying off in different directions. In spite of his many pragmatist corrections to and emendations of his hero Carnap, Quine could never bring into harmony his own scientific naturalism and residual empiricist hostility to modality.

V

According to this way of construing the tradition, Peirce initiated the American pragmatist school of philosophical thought already as a second Enlightenment, centered, as the first had been, on new conceptions of reason and models of intelligibility drawn from the best contemporary scientific achievements. Rorty thinks that Dewey added to the reconception of both knowers and the known that Peirce had bequeathed, a further substantial element inspired by and modeled on the first Enlightenment's principal advance in practical philosophy: its secularizing and humanizing disenchantment of traditional theologically based ethics. Peirce had provided a constructive alternative to the spectatorial picture of knowing as mirroring nature. But in his Girona period, Rorty draws from Dewey the leading idea and basic conceptual raw materials for a critique of Enlightenment philosophy's basic orienting representationalist semantic paradigm. He saw the critique he now envisaged as more radical and fundamental than the line he had pursued in *Philosophy and the Mirror of Nature*, where he had diagnosed that paradigm as inevitably precipitating a sterile oscillation between foundationalism and skepticism in epistemology. Astonishingly, Rorty would criticize the Enlightenment understanding of cognition in terms of representation as a politically objectionable form of authoritarianism. He took himself thereby to be following Dewey in turning the Enlightenment's own devastating practical critique of received religion against its own dominant theoretical strategy for under-standing cognition. Thought of this way, pragmatism as Rorty wants us to understand it just consists in following out the Enlightenment's own best insights and principal achievements to their logical conclusion, completing its humanistic transfor-mation of our philosophical self-conception.

The central strand of original Enlightenment thought that Rorty takes over as the fixed end of his analogy extends Kant's characterization in "Was ist Aufklärung?" The Enlightenment marks the ending of humanity's self-imposed tutelage, the achievement of our majority and maturity, for the first time taking adult responsibility for our own character and destiny. It is our emancipation from submission to the alien, nonhuman-because-superhuman authority of Old Nobodaddy in matters of our practical conduct. Henceforth we should deem it incompat-ible with our human dignity to understand ourselves as subject to any laws other than those we have in one way or another laid down for ourselves. No longer should our ideas about what is right and good be understood as having to have been dictated to us by a superhuman authority.

The deep Enlightenment insight was the diagnosis of what Marx, following Hegel, would later call "fetishism," concerning the practical norms we acknowledge and identify with as mak-ing us what we are. Fetishism is mistaking the products of our own practices and practical attitudes for features of the objective world that are what they are independent of and antecedent to those practices and attitudes. Marx's favorite example was the traditional conception of the *value* of precious metals, which thought of the value of metals the same way it thought of their density—so that there was, for instance, an *objectively* cor-rect answer to the question of how many ounces of silver are *really* worth as much as one ounce of gold.

The first Enlightenment, as Rorty construed it, concerned our emancipation from nonhuman authority in *practical* matters: issues of what we ought to do and how things ought to be. The envisaged second Enlightenment is to apply this basic lesson to our emancipation from nonhuman authority in *theoretical, cognitive* matters. Here the nonhuman authority in question is not that of God, but that of objective Reality—the philosophical conception Rorty liked to write with a capital R. In an essay published in English a few years after the Girona lectures, "Pragmatism as Anti-Authoritarianism," Rorty summarized the view he had announced there:[9]

> There is a useful analogy to be drawn between the pragmatists' criticism of the idea that truth is a matter of correspondence to the intrinsic nature of reality and the Enlightenment's criticism of the idea that morality is a matter of correspondence to the will of a Divine Being. The pragmatists' anti-representationalist account of belief is, among other things, a protest against the idea that human beings must humble themselves before something non-human, whether the Will of God or the Intrinsic Nature of Reality. (257)

He adds that "seeing anti-representationalism as a version of anti-authoritarianism permits one to appreciate an analogy that was central to John Dewey's thought," namely the analogy between ceasing to believe in Sin and ceasing to believe in Reality. The connection is:

> The representationalist tradition in philosophy which was dominant in those 400 years hoped that inquiry would put

---

[9] "Pragmatism as Anti-Authoritarianism," *Revue Internationale de Philosophie*, Vol. 53, No. 1, 207, 1999, pp. 7–20, and in John R. Shook and Joseph Margolis (eds), *A Companion to Pragmatism* (Oxford: Blackwell, 2006), pp. 257–266.

us in touch, if not with the eternal, at least with something which, in Bernard Williams's phrase, "is there anyway"—something non-perspectival, something which is what it is apart from human needs and interests. (263)

By contrast:

What Dewey most disliked about both traditional "realist" epistemology and about traditional religious beliefs is that they discourage us by telling us that somebody or something has authority over us. Both tell us that there is Something Inscrutable, something toward which we have duties, duties which have precedence over our cooperative attempts to avoid pain and obtain pleasure. (258)

Again:

Dewey was convinced that the romance of democracy, a romance built on the idea that the point of a human life is free cooperation with fellow humans, required a more thoroughgoing version of secularism than either Enlightenment rationalism or nineteenth-century positivism had achieved. As Dewey saw it, whole-hearted pursuit of the democratic ideal requires us to set aside *any* authority save that of a consensus of our fellow humans. (257)

Eduardo Mendieta says of the lesson of these lectures (in his introduction to *Take Care of Freedom and the Truth Will Take Care of Itself*[10]):

In the end, Rorty's adamant skepticism and anti-dogmatism are simply ways to be anti-authoritarian and irreverently anti-fetishistic. There is no supreme power that can offer an alibi,

[10] *Take Care of Freedom and the Truth Will Take Care of Itself: Interviews with Richard Rorty* (Stanford, CA: Stanford University Press, 2005).

warrant, or proof for our claims and beliefs, nothing except fallible human authority. There is no supreme authority, other than the authority of human justifications and reasons, whose only power is the power of persuasion.   (p. xvii)

Rorty's call for a second pragmatist Enlightenment, completing the first, is a Hegelian extrapolation of the original Kantian understanding of Enlightenment, extending the application of that conception from ethics to encompass also semantics and epistemology. Further on, I will say more about what makes it Hegelian, and what difference that step beyond Kant makes. But first it is worth filling in the argument behind this subsumption of semantic anti-*representationalism* under the banner of humanistic Enlightenment anti-*authoritarianism*. In its largest structure, I think it consists of two moves: a Kantian appreciation of the *normative* character of *representational* relations, and a Hegelian social *pragmatism* about *normativity* in general.

The first is part and parcel of Kant's radical recasting of Descartes's division of things into minds and bodies in terms of the distinction between norms and causes. Kant reconceives discursive intentionality (apperception or sapience) as a *normative* phenomenon. What principally distinguishes judgments and intentional actions from the responses of merely natural creatures is their normative status. Knowers and agents are *responsible* for how they take things to be and make things be. Candidate knowings and doings express *commitments* as to how things are or shall be. They are exercises of a distinctive kind of *authority*: the authority to commit oneself, to make oneself responsible. This is the authority to bind oneself by rules in the form of the concepts discursive beings apply in judging and intending. Merely natural creatures are bound by rules in the form of laws of nature. Discursive beings are bound by rules they bind themselves by: concepts they apply, which are rules determining what they have thereby made themselves responsible to and for. Their normative statuses (responsibilities, commitments) are instituted by their attitudes of undertaking or acknowledging those commitments. Autonomy is the essence of Kantian rationality. It is a distinctive normative sort of freedom, which Kant develops by turning Rousseau's definition of freedom—he says "obedience to a law one has prescribed for oneself is freedom"[11]—into a criterion of demarcation for genuinely *normative* bindingness.

As we have seen, one of the principal grounds on which in *Philosophy and the Mirror of Nature* Rorty condemns then contemporary analytic philosophy as still in thrall to Kantian conceptions is the central role Kant gives to the concept of *representation* in understanding the contentfulness of thought and experience. I think that in his later critique of representationalism in semantics on the basis of a more thoroughgoing and general version of Enlightenment anti-authoritarianism, Rorty follows Hegel in focusing on the *rulishness* of Kant's conception of representation. For Hegel reads Kant as offering a normative conception of *representation*, as a way of filling in his normative conception of *intentionality*. Kant dug down below Cartesian epistemological concerns about the warrant for our confidence in the *success* of our representational undertakings to uncover the underlying semantic understanding of representational *purport* they presuppose. Where Descartes takes for granted the representational purport of our thought (construing it as something we immediately know, just by having thoughts at all)—their being, in his phrase, *tanquam rem*, "as if of things"—Kant asks what it is about

[11] *Social Contract*, Book I, section 8, in Rousseau, Jean-Jacques, *The Social Contract and Other Later Political Writings*, trans. Victor Gourevitch (Cambridge: Cambridge University Press, 2018).

our thoughts in virtue of which they so much as *seem* to represent something else, purport to point beyond themselves to something they are of or about. One lesson that Hegel learns from Kant, as I understand him, is that a representing is *responsible* to what it represents for assessments of its correctness, in a distinctive sense. What is represent*ed* exercises *authority* over what count as represent*ings* of it just in virtue of its serving as a standard those representings are responsible to for such assessments of correctness (*as* representings). This is a radical reconceptualization of the representational relations between representeds and representings as a *normative* relation of authority and responsibility.

As I want to understand Rorty's late anti-representationalism as anti-authoritarianism argument, his long-standing *social pragmatism about normativity* comes into play because of this Hegelian *normative* understanding of representation, in terms of the authority of objective representeds over subjective representings of it. Pragmatism in this sense is the claim that normative statuses—paradigmatically responsibility or authority, commitment or entitlement—are always and everywhere features of the role something plays in social practices. Norms are creatures of our practices, instituted by our practical attitudes: how we take or treat things. Apart from their involvement in such practices, there are no *normative proprieties*, only *natural properties*.

This is a social, Hegelian version of a central Enlightenment idea. Samuel Pufendorf theorized about what he called the "imputation" of normative characteristics of things: the way they acquire this new sort of normative significance by playing a suitable role in our practices. Social contract theories of political obligation looked for the origins of normative statuses of political authority and responsibility in practical attitudes of contracting and consenting. By contrast to traditional ideas of an objective natural or supernatural order of normative superiority and subordination (the *scala natura*, the Great Chain of Being), the modern idea is that there were no statuses of authority and responsibility, no superiors and subordinates, until we started taking or treating each other *as* authoritative and responsible, *as* entitled to command and obliged to obey.

As I understand the course of his intellectual development, Rorty's axial commitment to social pragmatism about normativity, which becomes explicit in the 1970s, was a product of his invention of eliminative materialism in the 1960s. (That is why I described social pragmatism about normativity as a "long-standing" view of Rorty's.) As I would rationally reconstruct the chain of thought that emerged there, Rorty begins by thinking hard about the Cartesian conception of the mind, in connection with Wallace Matson's question: "Why Isn't the Mind-Body Problem Ancient?"[12] He focuses on what it is that thoughts and sense-impressions such as images have in common, that could have led Descartes to assimilate such different items under the specially crafted heading of "pensées"—an assimilation that would have seemed absurd to earlier Aristotelians, and to whose fraught consequences Sellars had sensitized him. The answer he eventually came to, starting off with the rough, popular characterization of "privacy" and ending with the substantially more focused notion of "incorrigibility," was in explicitly *normative* terms.[13] The key, he came to see, is a distinctive kind of first-person *authority*. Sincere contemporaneous first-person reports count as reports of *mental*

[12] In P. Feyerabend and G. Maxwell (eds), *Mind, Matter, and Method* (Minneapolis, MN: University of Minnesota Press, 1966), pp. 92–102.

[13] In "Mind-Body Identity, Privacy, and Categories," *The Review of Metaphysics*, Vol 19, No. 1, 1965, pp. 24–54, and "Incorrigibility as the Mark of the Mental," *The Journal of Philosophy*, Vol. LXVII, No. 12, 1970, pp. 399–424.

occurrences just in case and insofar as they have a distinctive kind of un-overrideable epistemic authority. We can't be either wrong about or ignorant of how things sensuously *seem* to us, or about what we are currently thinking, in the sense that no-one else's claims about *our* experience have the social significance of decisive objections to our sincere first-person avowals.

Understanding minds in the Cartesian sense accordingly shows up as the task of understanding the nature of that authority. One option is that the authority should be understood as a natural, objective, ontological feature of mental phenomena. But Rorty has learned from the later Wittgenstein to be suspicious of this idea. *Normative* statuses, he thinks, must ultimately be understood as *social* statuses. (This is a positive, Hegelian, pragmatist lesson Rorty learns from Dewey.) To talk about something as possessing authority is to talk about the role it plays in some social practice. Faced with two possible orders of explanation— from ontology to social practice (*attitudes* of acknowledging and attributing authority dispositionally reflect and normatively conform to antecedent objective normative *statuses*) and the other way around (normative *statuses* reflect the practical *attitudes* of participants in a social practice)—Rorty opts for the second. He is not prepared to think of the ancients as just having overlooked a key feature of the world: that nothing has the authority to contest sincere first-person reports of contemporaneous mental episodes. Rather, he thinks, social practices of according such authority to reports *changed*. Descartes both theoretically reflected and practically encouraged modern practical attitudes of taking or treating sincere first-person reports of contemporaneous mental events as having incorrigible authority. That change in normative attitudes brought into existence a new ontological category of thing: mental episodes as incorrigibly knowable by their possessors. It did that by instituting a differently structured set of normative statuses: a new kind of authority.

These two commitments—demarcating the ontological category of Cartesian mental events by the normative status of putatively cognitive attitudes toward them (claims reporting them) and understanding such normative statuses as instituted by social practices—together entailed that a change in practice of the same general sort that brought Cartesian minds into existence in the modern period could eliminate them going forward. This was Rorty's doctrine of "eliminative materialism." It made his academic career as an analytic philosopher. For it was (along with the contemporaneous *functionalism* of which it was a socially and normatively inflected variant) the first really original response to the mind-body problem in generations. It was the view in the philosophy of mind that corresponded to Nietzsche's historicist third way between theism and atheism (itself rooted in Hegel): there once was a God, but when our social practices and normative attitudes changed sufficiently, He died (it was by radically changing our practical attitudes that we killed Him). So eliminative materialism acknowledges that there have been and still are Cartesian minds, which are ontologically distinct from the merely material. But we brought those minds into existence by our practices, and by changing our practices could eliminate them and make materialism true.

Rorty acknowledged and embraced eliminative materialism as a pragmatist form of Hegelian historicism. In the "Pragmatism as Anti-Authoritarianism" essay I have been quoting from, he says "precisely because of his historicism, Dewey was, I believe, the classical pragmatist whose work will have the greatest utility in the long term."[14] This is an importantly correct characterization

[14] Rorty, "Pragmatism as Anti-Authoritarianism," in *A Companion to Pragmatism*, p. 260.

of Rorty's view. But I think it is equally important to understand that Rorty's *historicism* about Cartesian mindedness is argumentatively downstream from the social *pragmatism* about norms that emerges in his thought for the first time already in the 1960s. He is working with a distinction between two ontological categories of things, distinguished by the normative structure of authority that defines them. Cartesian mental things are what the attitudes of individuals have ultimate authority over, and social things (like discursive practices and the norms they institute) are what the attitudes of communities have ultimate authority over. And normative statuses such as authority and responsibility he classifies as social things. Because the ontological classification itself is defined in normative terms of authority structures, the category of the social, comprising the practices that institute all norms, is given pride of place as *primus inter pares*.

Rorty has considered and rejected *objectivism* about norms, and so about Cartesian mindedness. This is the idea that the presence or absence of things defined by the normative authority of individuals or of communities is an objective matter, in the sense of being independent of the practical attitudes of individuals or communities. In his eliminative materialism period, Rorty does not explicitly confront the status of this third ontological category of objective things: things about which neither individuals nor communities exercise final authority. The final stage of pragmatism construed as anti-authoritarianism, as the completion of a second Enlightenment, is the result of applying social pragmatism about normativity to the ontological realm of objective beings (what is objectively real) now themselves construed in normative terms of authority. According to Rorty's radicalized version of social pragmatism about norms, the very idea of objective things as exercising epistemic authority over our attitudes—underwritten by the *semantic* idea of represented serving as normative standards authoritative for assessments of the correctness of what count as representings of them just in virtue of being responsible to them for such assessments—is deeply and irremediably confused. *All* authority is in the end communal authority. Further, as we shall see, the critical function of reason as legitimating norms, as understood by the Enlightenment and made most fully explicit by Kant, teaches that we can only genuinely be responsible to *each other*, to what we can engage with in conversation, to what we can give justifying reasons *to* and in turn demand justifying reasons *from*.

This radicalization of social pragmatism about norms is now explicitly construed in *political* terms of freedom and dignity. "Only in a democratic society which describes itself in pragmatist terms, one can imagine Dewey saying, is the refusal to countenance any authority save that of consensus reached by free inquiry complete."[15] This is the standpoint from which growing out of acknowledging the overriding practical authority of an objective supernatural lawgiver and growing out of acknowledging the overriding cognitive authority of an objective natural represented reality come to seem to Rorty to be two sides of one coin. It is a lesson he takes himself to have learned from Hegel via Dewey:

> This is because he was the most historically minded: the one who learned from Hegel how to tell great sweeping stories about the relation of the human present to the human past. Dewey's stories are always stories of the progress from the need of human communities to rely on a non-human power to their realization that all they need is faith in themselves; they are stories about the substitution of fraternity for authority. His

[15] Rorty, "Pragmatism as Anti-Authoritarianism," in *A Companion to Pragmatism*, p. 265.

> stories about history as the story of increasing freedom are
> stories about how we lost our sense of sin, and also our hope of
> another world, and gradually acquired the ability to find the
> same spiritual significance in cooperation between finite
> mortals that our ancestors had found in their relation to an
> immortal being.[16]

The incipient pragmatist emancipation Rorty is working toward
is the substitution of a *pragmatics* of *consensus* for the *semantics* of
representation. All we can do is give and ask for reasons with each
other. Authority and responsibility are creatures of those discursive practices. We should accordingly reject the idea that our
discursive practices answer to, are responsible to, need to
acknowledge the authority of, anything outside those practices
and the practical attitudes of those who engage in them. The
constraint of the objective world on our practices should be
understood as exclusively *causal*, not *normative*. We are normatively constrained only by our reasons.

It is important to keep this contrast in mind. Like his hero
Dewey, Rorty never questioned the utility and importance of a
basically ecological concept of *reality* as the natural environment
with which we must cope and within which we must flourish as
biological organisms. This is the stubborn, recalcitrant reality
that causally constrains, challenges, frustrates, and rewards our
practical undertakings. The messy retail process of improving
our habits and attunements is, Rorty thinks, fully describable in
a wholly naturalistic vocabulary. What he objects to is the
philosophical concept he designates "Reality," distinguished by
the mock-honorific capital letter. This is the notion of something that has a distinctive kind of semantic and epistemic

---

[16] Rorty, "Pragmatism as Anti-Authoritarianism," in *A Companion to
Pragmatism*, p. 262.

authority over the correctness of our sayings and thinkings—reality as something we are responsible to in a way that transcends and constrains our linguistic social practices of giving and asking for reasons from without—just by objectively being what it is. The functional explanatory role that conception of reality plays, the status reality has with respect to us and our practices, is something that must be specified in *normative* terms.[17] There is no small irony in the absolutely central and essential role that the Kantian distinction between reasons and causes, norms and facts, plays in Rorty's thought. It is the overriding distinction that shapes his criticisms of the analytic philosophers he casts as twentieth-century neo-Kantians. He aims to use Kantian conceptual tools to undercut the Kantian conception of the philosophical project.

VI

This is a key point. Rorty's critique of representationalism is founded not on denying or ignoring the causal context in which our talk takes place and to which it ultimately *in some sense* answers, but precisely on a hard-headed insistence and focus upon the significance of that context. What distinguishes his view is rather his claim that the sense in which the talk answers to its environment must be understood *solely* in causal, rather than normative, terms—and his determination to follow out the

[17] I diagnose an unresolved tension between the Deweyan naturalism Rorty espouses in recommending naturalistic pragmatic metavocabularies and his Romantic appreciation of the transformative power of redescription (especially *self*-redescription) Rorty articulates in employing instead what I call his thoroughly normative "'vocabulary' vocabulary," in "Vocabularies of Pragmatism" in *Rorty and His Critics* (Oxford: Blackwell, 2000).

consequences of that claim wherever they lead. Rorty was always a Peircean naturalist, as I have sketched that notion above. He starts with the idea of us as natural creatures developing through learning habits that let us cope more or less well with our environments. We are guaranteed to "be in touch with the world" in the only sense that matters. For it is what we respond to and act in, our partner in pursuing Test-Operate-Test-Exit behavioral loops. To this Peircean selectional naturalism, which subsumes faster-cycling learning processes and slower-cycling evolutionary ones under the generic rubric of selectional "habit"-shaping mechanisms, Rorty sees Dewey as having usefully added an emphasis on the *social* character of practices that transcend individual learning processes. At this level, the "habits" that are cyclically shaped by ecological-adaptational causal interactions with the environment are in the first instance social practices. Individual dispositions are shaped and stabilized only in tandem with and mediated by those social practices. Rorty takes it that this broadened social naturalism (a "second-nature naturalism" as per McDowell in *Mind and World*) is endorsed also by the later Wittgenstein and the Heidegger of Division One of *Being and Time*. And Rorty himself goes beyond even Dewey, in making common cause with Wittgenstein in further focusing on specifically *discursive* practices: the deploying of what he calls "vocabularies." This is his pragmatism after the "linguistic turn."[18] The use of empirical vocabularies is held in place both causally and socially, by repeatable observation terms, whose application is keyed to the exercise of reliable differential responsive dispositions that

[18] This is, of course, the title of Rorty's 1967 anthology of classic philosophy of language papers, *The Linguistic Turn* (Chicago, IL: University of Chicago Press, 1967).

are sufficiently widely shared among the relevant members of the linguistic community—those who "agree in their use, upon concurrent stimulation," as Quine says in "Epistemology Naturalized."

At the core of the capacious "big tent" tradition Rorty retrospectively rationally reconstructs under the rubric of "pragmatism" is this broadly naturalistic, anthropological-ecological conception of language as an evolving population of discursive practices that is a, indeed the, distinctive feature of the natural history of creatures like us. That is what motivates and justifies his use of this term to characterize not only philosophers such as Peirce and Dewey, who embraced it themselves, but others such as Wittgenstein and Heidegger, and Sellars, Quine, and Davidson, who (sometimes explicitly and emphatically) did not. Rorty sees a stark contrast between this way of thinking about language and the analytic representationalist tradition that runs from Frege, Russell, and the Wittgenstein of the *Tractatus* through Carnap and Tarski to his colleague David Lewis. This tradition models language on formal monological logistical calculi, justification on proof of theorems from axioms, and truth conditions on model-theoretic semantics for such artificial languages. What, Rorty asks, does any of that have to do with what users of natural languages *do*? This opposition is epitomized in his slogan "Language is for coping, not copying."

In taking this line, Rorty rightly understands himself as appealing to the Peirce-Dewey tradition of American pragmatism to amplify and radicalize Quine's and Sellars's criticisms of Carnap, and following up on Wittgenstein's advice for philosophers to look not to the meaning of expressions, but to their use. Rorty sometimes seems to draw the lesson that we should do pragmatics instead of semantics (which he identifies with appeals to the notions of *truth* and *representation*), study use rather than meaning. When talking this way, he is following the later Wittgenstein (who recoils from his semantics-only Tractarian view to a pragmatics-only approach), James, and Dewey, but not Peirce, Sellars, Quine, and Davidson. They should be understood as pursuing pragmatics-first, rather than semantics-first explanatory strategies, but not as trading the traditional neglect of pragmatics by the representationalist semantic tradition for a corresponding pragmatist dismissal of semantics *holus bolus*. I think that another genuine strand in Rorty's thought belongs in this tradition. He does have views about meaning. But he thinks we should understand it in terms of justificatory practices rather than a notion of *truth* understood in terms of representation. This contrast is important for the lessons I want to draw about the concept of *representation* from Hegel's treatment of it in the *Phenomenology*, in the second part of this work. So it is worth looking a little bit more closely at how Rorty does think about meaning in the context of discursive social practices. For here we see both a subtle interplay and perhaps a residual tension between pragmatist naturalism and an insistence on a Kantian disjunction between norms and causes in Rorty's views in the vicinity.

Rorty inscribes within his Peircean, broadly naturalistic account, a distinction between the social-normative and the nonsocial, so non-normative, merely natural world of vocabulary-less things. The norms that articulate vocabulary use are to be understood functionally, in terms of roles in social practices that include the adoption of normative attitudes. Practitioners adopt such attitudes by taking or treating each other in practice *as* committed or entitled, responsible or authoritative. In the sort of pragmatics-first order of explanation he recommends, we think of what one is doing in claiming, say, that the frog is on the log, as undertaking a commitment. Doing that is taking up a stance in a normative space, acquiring a distinctive kind of social status. Rorty understands such statuses ultimately in terms of interpersonal practices of justification. In adopting normative stances we make ourselves answerable to each other for doing so. We are liable to be challenged, and obliged to defend the normative statuses we claim. One commitment is treated by community members as providing a *reason for* another, as providing a justification for it, when it successfully performs this function of vindicating entitlement to the challenged commitment.

The meaning expressed by using some bit of vocabulary is to be understood in terms of the role it plays in these practices of giving and practically assessing reasons: what its application provides reasons for and against and what provides reasons for and against its application. All there is to confer meaning on our noises is the role they play in our practices of taking up, challenging, and defending the stances taken up by applying them. (These justificatory practices include and are constrained by claims practitioners find themselves with as a result of exercising noninferential, reliable, differential, responsive dispositions to endorse observational claims,—those that community members largely agree about "under concurrent stimulation.") Understanding meaning or semantic content in terms of inferential roles read off of justificatory practices is a way of implementing the pragmatics-first order of explanation without giving up on semantics.

Rorty thinks such a pragmatist explanatory strategy can underwrite unobjectionable kinds of truth-talk. We just have to restrict ourselves to properties of truth that can be cashed out in pragmatic terms of what we are doing in *taking* or *treating* something *as* true. Committing oneself to the claim that the frog is on the log by asserting the sentence "The frog is on the log" *is* taking it to be true that the frog is on the log. This is the thought that lies behind such Rortyan formulations as that the truth is just whatever planks in Neurath's boat the community is currently leaving alone—or, more provokingly, "the truth is whatever your community will let you get away with." Such intentionally outrageous formulations invite the attribution to Rorty of a social-linguistic version of the sort of ludicrous subjective idealism associated with "the god-intoxicated Berkeley/who proved all things a dream/that this great farrowing pig of a world/that doth so solid seem/would vanish in an instant if the mind but change its theme." It is important to realize that any such imputation presupposes a pre-Quinean, pre-Wittgensteinian picture according to which the meanings of the noises linguistic practitioners use are somehow fixed determinately in advance of any question of how they are actually used. Once the meanings are fixed, it is of course nonsense to think the community can in general make true whatever sentences it likes simply by practically taking or treating them as true. But our words do not mean what they mean apart from which sentences involving them we actually take to be true. Rorty introduces the "vocabulary" vocabulary precisely to acknowledge the Quinean and Wittgensteinian point that actual practices of using expressions—adopting commitments and treating some of them as reasons for or against others—are all there is to determine the contents expressed by using noises and marks (what Sellars calls "sign designs" and Wittgenstein epitomizes as the sign-post "considered just as a piece of wood").

Making It Explicit offers Rorty two ways in which his justification-first pragmatic approach to truth might be improved, consonant with his own pragmatist scruples. First, instead of thinking of truth Peirce-wise, in terms of consensus, we can think about it in social-perspectival terms of the pragmatics of knowledge ascriptions. The idea is to think about what practitioners are *doing* in taking someone to know something. We just need to transpose the traditional justified true belief (JTB) account into a pragmatic key (putting aside for these purposes Gettier-type worries about the ultimate sufficiency of these conditions). To take someone to know something one must do three things. To begin with, one attributes a belief. In the normative vocabulary I have been using to codify Rorty's views, this is attributing a distinctive kind of normative status: a discursive commitment. Next, one takes that stance or status to be justified: one the candidate knower is entitled to. What one is doing in taking that justified commitment one attributes to be, in addition, true should not be understood as attributing to it some further property (which would most naturally be thought of in representational terms). Rather, what one must do to take it to be true is endorse oneself: undertake oneself the same commitment or endorsement one attributes and takes the other to be justified in adopting. If one does not appreciate the fundamental distinction of social perspective between *attributing* a commitment to another and *undertaking* that commitment oneself, one will be tempted to assimilate taking-true to attributing commitment and entitlement. Making that mistake then requires metaphysical extravagance in explaining the peculiar features of *what* one attributes. It is just this picture that pragmatists rightly reject. Understanding things this way justifies Rorty's endorsement of James's formula that truth is what is right in the way of belief.

One way Rorty liked to put his deflationary attitude toward truth is by characterizing truth an "empty compliment" that we can pay to someone's belief or utterance. In such formulations "empty" does not entail that there is no important distinction to be made between beliefs we are prepared to pay that compliment to and those we are not. That difference is just the difference between beliefs we agree with and those we do not—and that is a distinction of some practical importance. He means that this pragmatic significance does not reflect some deeper metaphysical property we are taking beliefs to have when we pay them this compliment. A second friendly amendment I offered is then a deflationary account of truth-talk that I take to be more expressively adequate to the variety of forms such talk can take. In particular, pragmatists about truth owe an explanation of uses of "true" that occur as components of more complicated assertibles. When I say "If what the representationalist says in the passage at the top of page 17 is true, then pragmatism is in trouble," I have not endorsed or agreed with the offending remark. Redundancy and disquotationalist approaches to truth-talk extend to these unasserted, embedded uses, as well as the free-standing endorsement-indicating ones. The most sophisticated and technically adequate theory of this sort, in my view, is anaphoric, prosentential accounts, according to which sentences such as "that is true" inherit their content from their anaphoric antecedents (what the representationalist says in the passage at the top of page 17, or whatever utterance "that" refers to). I elaborate an account of this sort in *Making It Explicit* and elsewhere.[19] The details don't matter here.

Rorty enthusiastically embraced both these ways of filling in his account of how pragmatists should think about truth. These sorts of accounts of truth-talk—the social-perspectival story on the side of force and the prosentential story on the side of

[19] Chapter 5 of *Making It Explicit*, and "Expressive vs. Explanatory Deflationism about Truth" In *What Is Truth?*, edited by Richard Schantz (Berlin: Hawthorne de Gruyter, 2002), pp. 103–119. Reprinted in *Deflationary Truth*, edited by Bradley P. Armour-Garb and J.C. Beall (Chicago, IL: Open Court, 2005), pp. 237–257.

content—are all right from his point of view because they take their places within a functionalist understanding of meaning based on justification rather than truth. The meaning of a sentence is a matter of the role it plays in justificatory practices. Those practices of giving and asking for reasons are construed as the distinctively semantogenic aspect of the use of the sentence. Situated inside such a pragmatist use-in-justification-first order of explanation, truth-talk is explained in terms of its distinctive expressive role, which can be seen to be parasitic on the meanings sentences acquire in virtue of their role in justificatory practices. So understood, the concept of truth does not play any fundamental explanatory role in semantics of the sort epitomized by truth-conditional accounts of meaning, which address justification only late in the story, if at all.

By focusing to begin with on justification, rather than truth, Rorty not only opens up a path from pragmatics to semantics (theorizing about use to theorizing about meaning), but also carves out a distinctively *normative* space within the broadly naturalistic Peircean pragmatist picture in which he is framing his account. This is important because, as we shall see, his Girona-era criticism of representationalism turns precisely on its inability to make sense of the sort of semantic norms it presupposes. In this way, Rorty turns the axial Kantian distinction between normative questions (the "Quid juris?" question) and objective factual ones (the "Quid facti?" question) back on Kant's most basic semantic concept: representation. He does so by combining another Kantian idea with the Hegelian understanding of normative statuses as ultimately social statuses. Rorty fully endorses and exploits Kant's distillation of the Enlightenment lesson, that what distinguishes *rational authority* (normative constraint) from mere compulsion (causal constraint) is liability to criticism, in the sense of answerability to demands for *reasons* for the exercise of that authority. In this sense, we can only answer to each other: to those who give and demand reasons. That means that only those who engage in justificatory practices can exercise the distinctive Kantian authority to commit oneself, to make oneself responsible by adopting an attitude or performing an act (theoretically, by judging, or practically, by endorsing a practical maxim). Normative statuses are conferred by, are products of, justificatory social practices. Far from being an irrationalist, by pursuing this line of thought Rorty puts reasoning at the center of human life. He uses justificatory practices of giving reasons and critical practices of demanding them at the center of his version of the Kantian distinction between merely natural beings, who are bound by laws, and normative beings (natural only in a broader sense that includes their social practices), who are bound also by their conceptions of laws, conceptually articulated by rules specifying what is a reason for what. By insisting on the essentially social character of the rational, critical, and justificatory practices within which performances acquire genuinely normative significance, Rorty knowingly takes a giant step toward a Hegelian understanding of that Kantian distinction between us and it.

VII

Rorty was probably the most polarizing philosophical figure of his generation. I believe that the conclusion of the line of thought I have been rehearsing, distilled by him over four decades, is the root cause of the stark division into opposing camps of rabid Rortyphobes and adoring Rortyphiles. It is, of course, iconoclastic to attack the modern picture of the mind as the mirror of nature, to seek to dethrone the dominant representational conception of our cognitive relations to the world. But semantic representationalism, pervasive and philosophically powerful though it might be, is pretty dry stuff, of interest principally to specialists. So, too, is the "crisis" of epistemological foundationalism, which Rorty saw as its unlovely offspring. What arouses passion, I think, is the consequent rejection of the very idea of *objective reality* as what it is the point of our practices to represent—which Rorty sees as following from his critique of the semantic concept of *representation*. Further, when we jettison that representational semantic model, along with it, he thinks, must go the idea of our cognitive practices as *rational* in the specific sense that essentially incorporates the goal of *fidelity* to the objective, attitude-independent *facts*. But it is important at this point not to lose sight of the fact that he rejects representational semantic models on behalf of the ideals of reason, freedom, and democracy. For Rorty does so on behalf of a *humanized*, nonrepresentational conception of rationality as consisting of responsiveness to *reasons* providing norms governing our practice, not to be confused with the merely causal constraint on our conduct exercised by our nonhuman environment (which he never dreamed of denying).

From the point of view of his critics, however, it is bad enough that in place of the lofty ideal of science as a practical method for getting it right concerning how things anyway are, Rorty wants to put a purposely low-key notion of "coping" or "muddling through." But when he further construes giving and asking for reasons, assessing evidence, justifications, and explanations, as all ultimately and ineluctably a matter of *politics*—his strong reading of James's claim that "The trail of the human serpent is over all"—the gauntlet has been thrown down and battle joined. (At this point the Deweyan insistence that what is envisaged is *democratic* politics defining ourselves by the result of exercises of our freedom to give and ask each other for reasons is unlikely to reassure or change minds.) This, the critics claim, is gross, dangerous irrationalism.

There are weighty considerations available on this side of the dialectic. For it can be claimed that Rorty recklessly proposes to sacrifice a precious legacy of the actual Enlightenment: its appreciation of natural science as the very form of knowledge, as the disinterested pursuit of truth by the impartial assessment of reasons grounded in empirical evidence and answerable to how things really, objectively, anyway are. The sharp contrast between this cognitive scientific enterprise and every sort of *merely* political wrangling can be thought of as *the* essential insight of the Enlightenment.[20] The correctness of its realistic, objectivist theoretical understanding of both empirical science and the world it seeks rationally to comprehend is vouched for daily by the practical success of its technological arm, the engine of the Industrial Revolution, which has made natural science the most staggeringly successful social institution of the last 300 years. That very success was, of course, the principal *datum* for Peirce's pragmatist proposal for completing the Enlightenment.

At this point the stage is set for both for assessing Rorty's argument on the model of *modus tollens* rather than *modus ponens*, and for using one's attitude toward it as a touchstone for assessing one's philosophical temperament as tough- or tender-minded—or even as hard- or soft-headed. Rorty was always both struck and bemused by the extent to which the issue

---

[20] Jacques Bouveresse eloquently articulates this complaint (in a friendly, intramural spirit) in his contribution "Reading Rorty: Pragmatism and Its Consequences," in *Rorty and His Critics*, edited by Robert B. Brandom (Oxford: Blackwell, 2000), pp. 129–145.

presented itself to his opponents as a *moral* one—as a choice between good and evil. This aspect of the debate on the theoretical side of cognition seemed to him to mirror exactly that on the practical side of action. The foes of the original Enlightenment could not understand how anyone who denied the authority of God to determine right and wrong concerning actions, independently of human attitudes, could nonetheless be a good person, concerned about acting as one ought. The foes of Rorty's projected second Enlightenment cannot understand how anyone who denies the authority of objective facts to determine right and wrong beliefs, independently of human attitudes, could nonetheless recognize a distinction between better and worse arguments: genuine reasons for and against claims. Rorty said that he looked forward to a time when this criticism would seem as quaint and odd to people as the evident moral depravity of anyone who believed that the principle of motion of material bodies could be understood without looking outside the natural realm of those material bodies to their supernatural causes seems to us now.

Rorty faced with characteristic honesty, clarity, and fortitude the question raised by taking his line of argument to what he saw as its necessary conclusion. One can debate, with him and on his behalf, just how bad things would be if we were forced to put the idea of an objective nonhuman reality represented by and serving as the ultimate authority over the correctness of our empirical beliefs into a box with the idea of a supernatural nonhuman being whose will has ultimate authority over the correctness of our moral beliefs. And one can debate the propriety of treating the badness of such a conclusion, which is to force an understanding of his argument as appropriately exploiting the implication he points to contrapositively, rather than, as he does, by detaching the conclusion. But if one rejects Rorty's conclusion—whether because of its consequences or simply because one cannot deal with its outrageous radicality—one then owes a diagnosis of where the argument for it has gone astray. Where, exactly, does the analogy between the anti-authoritarianism of the first Enlightenment on practical matters and the anti-authoritarianism of Rorty's projected second Enlightenment on cognitive matters break down?

Is the difference that makes a difference the difference in directions of fit? In Anscombe's anecdote illustrating the difference between practical and theoretical reason, the shopper consulting a list and filling a shopping basket accordingly epitomizes the practical direction of fit and the detective writing a list of what the shopper puts in the basket epitomizes the cognitive direction of fit. In the context of assessing Rorty's argument, it is critical to appreciate that these complementary directions of fit are characterized in *normative* terms. If what is on the list does not correspond to what is in the basket, in the shopper's case what is in the basket is incorrect and in the detective's case what is on the list is incorrect. For the list is *authoritative* in the first case: the shopper is obliged to follow the standard it provides, is responsible to it, for assessments of the correctness of what he puts in the basket. And the basket is authoritative in the second case: the detective is obliged to follow the standard it provides, is responsible to it, for what she puts on her list. Rorty's social pragmatism about norms (downstream from Dewey and the later Wittgenstein) construes all these statuses of authority and responsibility as roles, lists, and baskets, shoppers and detectives, play in social practices that institute those normative significances. That much is common to the practical and cognitive directions of fit just because they are directions of *normative* fit: a matter of the socially instituted location of standards for normative assessments of correctness.

Rather than undercutting Rorty's analysis, invocation of Anscombian direction of fit seems to support and confirm the analogy he relies on in projecting the need for a second Enlightenment to complete on the cognitive side the anti-authoritarian work the first accomplishes on the practical side. For Anscombe, too, focuses on the essentially normative significance of the *representational* semantic dimension of doxastic or epistemic relations. That is enough to give Rorty's social pragmatism about norms a grip and prepare the ground for his anti-authoritarian claim that objectivizing or naturalizing those essentially normative representational relations, reifying epistemically authoritative represented facts or reality, is falling into fetishism.

As I have reconstructed it, the two pillars supporting Rorty's final global anti-representationalist argument are the *normative construal of representational relations* as essentially involving the authority of representeds over what count as representings of them just in virtue of their responsibility to those representeds, which serve as standards for assessments of the correctness of the representings (in a distinctive, representation-constitutive sense of "correctness"), and the *social pragmatism about norms* that consists in understanding all normative statuses (paradigmatically, authority and responsibility) as conferred by or consisting in roles in social practices. I take it that both express genuine and important insights: the first Kantian, and the second Hegelian. But I also think that a closer look at these two ideas opens up room for a nonfetishistic view that is friendlier to the concept of *representation*, and so more like the one I was championing in the Girona three-way than the one Rorty was defending. In particular, I think it is possible to understand empirical discursive commitments as representing objective facts (concerning objective properties and relations of particulars), to understand the representational relations those commitments stand in to what is represented as essentially and not just accidentally a normative matter of authority and responsibility, and to understand those normative statuses as instituted by social practices. Further, I think Hegel himself shows us in detail how to do that.

The basic issue is how to understand social pragmatism about norms. The underlying idea is that normative statuses are ultimately social statuses. Normative significances, such as having authority or being responsible, are instituted or conferred by playing a distinctive kind of role in social practices. Both Hegel and the Wittgenstein of the *Investigations*, each in his own way, developed and exploited this idea (as, indeed, arguably, did the Heidegger of Division One of *Being and Time*[21]). Drawing Rorty's conclusion requires a stronger version of this thought, however. For Rorty takes it that it follows from social pragmatism about norms in this sense that nothing *nonhuman* can exercise authority over us, that we cannot be responsible to any nonhuman authority. His reason, I think, is that discursive authority and responsibility are *rational* authority and responsibility—in the sense of being normative statuses that matter for practices of giving and asking for *reasons*. What doesn't make a difference for those practices is semantically inert and epistemically irrelevant. And we have already emphasized that it is a key Enlightenment insight, emphasized, distilled, and developed in Kant's critical philosophy, that authority is rational authority only insofar as it involves a correlative justificatory responsibility—a responsibility to provide *reasons* for exercising that authority in one way or on one occasion rather than another.

---

[21] Cf. Robert B. Brandom, "Heidegger's Categories in *Being and Time*," chapter 10 of *Tales of the Mighty Dead* (Cambridge, MA: Harvard University Press, 2002).

Rorty thinks that nothing that cannot fulfill that justificatory responsibility should be understood to exercise genuine authority within and according to our reason-giving practices. We should acknowledge the authority only of what we can critically interrogate as to its reasons. Only what can fulfill its critical rational responsibility to give reasons justifying the exercise of that authority should count as having genuine authority. He concludes that only parties to our conversations, only participants in our practices, can have normative statuses. In the end, the only authority we ought to recognize is each other: those to whom we owe reasons for our commitments and those who owe such justifying reasons to us for exercises of their authority. *Rational* authority involves a correlative *justificatory* responsibility. To attribute such normative statuses to anything that can't talk is to fetishize. It is for this reason that the supposed authority of a nonhuman God and a nonhuman represented Reality are alike condemned as ultimately irrational, fetishistic remnants of traditional conceptions, which it is the task, the privilege, and the glory of Enlightenment to sweep away. It shows how little many of his critics have understood Rorty's arguments that a principal charge in their indictment of him is his supposed "irrationalism." On the contrary, it is precisely his devotion to reason and its essential critical function in making normative statuses genuinely binding—the great Enlightenment discovery—that drives this whole line of thought. He is trying to think through rigorously what reason is and what it requires of us.

At the base of this argument is a new principle, which builds on but goes beyond social pragmatism about normative statuses. Its slogan is "No (genuine) authority without (rational) responsibility." I think there is something deeply right about it. Some version of this thought is central not only to Kant's understanding of us discursive beings as essentially autonomous, but also to what Hegel made of that autonomy idea. For Kant, the basic normative status (our dignity as autonomous, which others are obliged practically to respect) is having the *authority* to make ourselves *responsible*, to commit ourselves. Committing ourselves (making ourselves responsible) *cognitively*, to how things are, is judging: endorsing a proposition. Committing ourselves (making ourselves responsible) *practically*, to how things are to be, is willing or intending: endorsing a practical maxim or principle. Among the things one makes oneself responsible for *doing* by exercising discursive authority of either the cognitive or the practical variety is providing *reasons* that justify undertaking or acknowledging the commitments one does. Exercising one's authority as autonomous makes one vulnerable to assessments of one's reasons for those exercises. This is Kant's distillation and development of the lessons of Enlightenment.

It is more than a little ironic that when Rorty later sought new arguments for the global anti-representationalism he had first defended in *Mirror*, he once again turned to Kant, the archrepresentationalist villain of that book. But what he turned to is one key principle animating Kant's political liberalism—forging a connection between legitimate authority, the responsibility for reasoned justification, and democracy that Rorty whole-heartedly applauds in the form that Dewey later gave it. The later Rorty is entirely comfortable with mounting an argument against semantic representationalism and the conception of epistemically authoritative represented reality it articulates that is ultimately a *political* argument, even if it relies on ideas whose credentials can be traced back to Kant. (Rorty's disagreements with Habermas's more transcendental Kantian political liberalism, in favor of his own less metaphysical Deweyan political liberalism, are intramural. What he objects to about Kant is not his liberal politics.) As I am reconstructing Rorty's argument, two of the three principal premises of his anti-authoritarian argument for global anti-representationalism and rejection of the idea of reality as the object of representation that it involves are due ultimately to Kant: the normative analysis of representational relations and the idea that genuine authority involves a correlative responsibility to be responsive to critical demands for reasons. The third pole in the tripod, social pragmatism about normative statuses such as authority and responsibility, was introduced by Hegel rather than Kant.

I think Kant is right that the most basic sort of normative status is a kind of authority that is rational and rationally binding just insofar as it essentially involves correlative justificatory responsibility to provide reasons for its exercise. Hegel follows him on this point. Unless there were normative statuses of this sort, there would be no norms at all. But I do not think that *all* authority must be of this fundamental kind. Once implicitly normative social practices are up and running, derivative sorts of normative statuses, parasitic on the basic ones that characterize discursive practitioners, become possible. It is true that, as social pragmatism about normative statuses has it, it is only in virtue of playing a suitable role in social practices that anything acquires specifically normative significance. And it is true that those practices must include the special kind of role practitioners can play, in virtue of which they have the authority to commit themselves, to make themselves responsible to each other—among other things, but essentially, responsible for giving each other *reasons* justifying the commitments they have undertaken by exercising their authority. But in the context of discursive practices that include the kinds of authority characteristic of us as reason-giving-and-assessing participants, those interlocutors can confer other, parasitic sorts of normative significance on things that are not themselves capable of giving and asking for reasons.

Consider omens and oracles. A community can have practices according to which if a flock of black birds flies over the group that is deciding whether to undertake a momentous risky action—planting the crops this early in the season, making or breaking an alliance, moving the tribe to a new location—that natural event is accorded the normative significance of a bad portent. It can in practice be accorded the authority to prohibit the course of action in question. It only has that normative significance in virtue of the practical attitudes of the community members, who *make* it authoritative by *taking* it to be authoritative, by treating it *as* an ominous sign. There is nothing mysterious about how natural occurrences can come to be accorded such significances. Even if the practitioners are fetishists in their meta-attitudes—in that they deny the efficacy of their own practices in instituting the normative significance in question, taking it to be an objective, broadly natural, or supernatural matter of fact—nonetheless *we* can see that they do in fact confer that normative significance by how they treat natural events of this kind, just as social pragmatism about norms claims. They are acting so as to grant authority over their own decisions to the occurrence or nonoccurrence of certain natural phenomena. And although the practitioners must be able to ask and offer each other reasons for their commitments—for instance, to cite the appearance of the birds as a reason not to break the alliance—it need not be possible to ask the birds for reasons for exercising the authority that has been attributed to them. There need be nothing that counts as holding the birds responsible for the decision their behavior authorized or prohibited in order for their authority to be intelligible as socially instituted or "imputed."

Social pragmatism about norms says that the practices of the community are the *fons et origo* from which all normative significance flows. But that is compatible with those practices conferring normative significance, for instance, the status of having authority, on things other than the reason-mongering community members whose practices they are. And though the authority of those practitioners to participate in the practices that confer such significances essentially, and not just accidentally, involves correlative responsibilities, including those that involve liability to demands for reasons for their exercise of that authority, the same need not hold of all the items to which they attribute normative significance, including various kinds of authority over aspects of their practice ("No rum while the sun is over the yardarm"). So the three principles I have excavated as the basis of Rorty's argument, when properly understood, leave room for the possibility that our discursive practices can confer on objective things and occurrences the normative significance of serving as standards for assessment of the correctness of what count as representings of them just in virtue of being in that sense responsible for their correctness to how it objectively is with what thereby counts as represented by them. That is conferring on representeds a distinctive kind of authority over representings. Participants in a practice granting authority over various aspects of that practice to things that are not even candidates for first-class status as participants (in virtue of their ineligibility as reason-givers) might in particular cases be unwise—as it surely is for treating the vagaries of birds as action-licensing or action-prohibiting omens, and could well be for letting the sun's position determine when rum rations are due and appropriate. But it is neither unintelligible on social pragmatist grounds nor incompatible with our dignity as rational members of a democratic polity. The important point remains that nonhuman things can have only the authority *we* grant them.

If that is right, then these considerations lead to what is essentially a problem in social engineering. Once we see that the possibility is not ruled out in principle, we must ask whether there is a structure or configuration of practices that deserves to count as granting to things specifically *representational* authority over our thought and talk. How should we understand such authority, and what, exactly, do we need to do to institute it or confer it on things we will then qualify as thinking and talking *about*? More pointedly, can we make sense of our attitudes as having representational content in a sense that grants authority over their correctness to "how things anyway are"—where "anyway" means independence *in some sense*, of our attitudes, including those that instituted the normative representational relations in the first place? For on the normative tripartite ontological sorting of things into subjective, social, and objective that emerged from Rorty's arguments for eliminative materialism, to represent objective things is to represent things about whose properties neither individual attitudes nor community attitudes are finally authoritative. Rather, authority must be granted to, practically taken to reside in and be exercised by, the things themselves. Explaining how that possibility—which I have argued is left open in principle by the three principles on which Rorty's representationalism-as-fetishism argument against the very idea of *objective reality* is based—can actually be realized in practice is a tall order and a hard job.

I think Hegel offers just such an account. He subscribes to, and his account respects and accords with, all three of the principles Rorty invokes: social pragmatism about norms, the idea that representational relations between representeds and representings must be understood in normative terms of authority and responsibility, and an understanding of the most basic normative statuses as necessarily involving critical rational responsibility to give reasons correlative with any imputed authority. In my second lecture I will explain how I think Hegel's story about the institution of normative representational relations goes. At the heart of his explanation is the idea that the relations between norms (normative statuses such as authority and responsibility) and the normative attitudes that both institute and answer to those norms, is essentially *historical*. In the end, I want to claim, Rorty did not follow his line of thought all the way through to its proper conclusion because he (following Dewey) did not sufficiently appreciate the thorough-going nature of Hegel's historicism, and the remarkable and distinctive conception of specifically *recollective* rationality it articulates. That is the topic of my next lecture.

Lecture 2

RECOGNITION AND RECOLLECTION

The Social and Historical Dimensions of Reason

I

In my first lecture I talked about the evolution of Rorty's arguments against semantic representationalism, to its final, mature form. The key concept of that late constellation of concerns was *authoritarianism*. (Recall that the title Rorty chose for the projected book version of his late, definitive Girona lectures, published posthumously, was *Pragmatism as Anti-Authoritarianism*.) Authoritarianism is an attitude toward the relations between normative statuses and critical practices of giving and asking for reasons. It consists in practically or theoretically taking it that there can be genuine authority without a corresponding *critical* responsibility to give *reasons* entitling one to that authority and to particular exercises of it. Social practices are authoritarian to the extent that they decouple normative statuses from issues of rational legitimation, treating authority as not in principle liable to rational challenge and in need of rational

Pragmatism and Idealism: Rorty and Hegel on Reason and Representation. Robert B. Brandom, Oxford University Press. © Robert B. Brandom 2022. DOI: 10.1093/oso/9780192870216.003.0002

defense. *Fetishism* is the traditional form of authoritarianism. If and insofar as norms—paradigmatically the statuses of superiority and subordination, the right to command and the responsibility to obey that structure the Great Chain of Being—are just objective matters of fact (whether natural or supernatural, but in either case independent of the social practices and practical attitudes of those subject to those norms), they are beyond rational challenge and the need for rational defense. As aspects of how things simply are, they are immune to critical exercises of reason. Rorty's claim is that although the Enlightenment got past fetishistic authoritarianism in its understanding of practical moral norms, it remained mired in such a view when it came to specifically representational norms on the theoretical, cognitive side. I will claim in this lecture that Rorty's social pragmatism about norms is what Hegel takes to be the essence of distinctively *modern* views of normativity. It is possible to take this lesson on board and still deny critical rational accountability for the norms communities institute by their practices. Seeing norms as instituted (solely) by power relations—the essence of *fascism* ("might makes right")—is authoritarianism that has both traditional fetishistic forms and forms that are modern in Hegel's sense.

Rorty takes it that Kant was right to draw from his distillation of the insights of the Enlightenment the lesson that genuine norms essentially involve liability to rational criticism, to demands for reasons justifying and legitimizing claims to authority. Rorty's argument for the need to complete the work of the Enlightenment by rejecting Kant's program of understanding cognition in terms of the master-concept of *representation* proceeds by turning Kant's critical insight against Kant's own representational model. For Rorty sees that *representation* is a normative concept. This is an idea Hegel, too, finds in Kant. Something plays the functional role of a representing just insofar as it is responsible to what counts as represented by it in virtue of exercising the authority over that representing that consists in what is represented serving as a normative standard for assessments of the *correctness* of the representing *as* a representing *of* that represented. But Rorty takes it that it is a consequence of Kant's good Enlightenment idea that there is no genuine authority without critical rational responsibility that we can only be genuinely responsible to each other—to those to whom we can address rational challenges and from whom we can demand reasons defending their claimed authority and its particular exercises. The idea that inanimate objects and objective states of affairs can exercise representational authority over the beliefs of those who *can* engage in critical rational challenges and defenses is a remnant of fetishistic authoritarianism. Not only are normative statuses instituted by social practices—which is the thesis of social pragmatism about norms—but those social practices essentially and not just accidentally include practices of giving and asking for reasons. In taking this additional step Rorty shows himself to be a distinctive kind of *rationalist* about norms: a Kantian *critical* rationalist. (It should be acknowledged that this way of putting things runs counter to Rorty's own rhetorical preferences and practice.) So Rorty uses Kant against Kant, to argue that we should no more recognize the authority of what we cannot converse with and interrogate as to its reasons in the cognitive, theoretical aspects of our discursive practice (as he takes it the representational model requires) than we should in the practical, moral aspects of that practice.

In this lecture, I argue for two claims. The first is that the considerations and commitments that shape the final, antiauthoritarian argument of Rorty's that I reconstructed in the first lecture are among the central concerns Hegel addresses in his *Phenomenology*. The second is that Hegel there assembles and deploys conceptual resources that suffice to disarm Rorty's anti-authoritarian arguments against the legitimacy and ultimate intelligibility of the concept of *representation*. Hegel offers a *social, historical, expressivist* account of the process by which the normative authority of represented over representings, and the corresponding responsibility of representings to representeds, are instituted by communities engaged in discursive practices with the right structure.[1] I think Rorty accepts the first point, and that that is largely why he saw Hegel (at least, in a Deweyan, suitably naturalized form) as representing a way forward for philosophy that contrasts with the ultimately blind alley into which, in *Philosophy and the Mirror of Nature*, he argues Kant had led us. But I do not think he ever was in a position to appreciate the second point.

Rorty does appreciate and applaud Hegel's development of Kant's account of conceptual normativity by understanding it as articulated along two dimensions that were not central to Kant's conception: the social and the historical. He also realized that Hegel endorsed Kant's anti-authoritarian, critical insight into the essential dependence of genuine authority on its legitimation by engagement in the dialogical (dialectical) cut-and-thrust of rational challenge and defense. He was, I think, like not a few of Hegel's readers, a bit hazy about exactly how that critical insight is supposed to be integrated into the equally progressive picture of conceptual norms as socially instituted and historically evolving.

---

[1] The story I tell here—and in particular the account of Hegel's conception of recollective rationality, which is the key to the expressive analysis of the representational dimension of conceptual content—is developed in much greater detail in my book *A Spirit of Trust: A Reading of Hegel's* Phenomenology (Cambridge, MA: Harvard University Press, 2019), to which this discussion may be considered an introduction.

If we delve into the next level of fine structure in Hegel's constructive account, we see him introducing two crucial structural conceptions. The social character of conceptual norms is understood according to a distinctive new model: normative statuses such as authority and responsibility are instituted by reciprocal recognitive attitudes. The historical character of conceptual norms is also understood according to a distinctive new model: the content of conceptual norms is determined by expressively progressive processes of recollective rationalization of attitudes actually adopted by practitioners. *Recognition* is Hegel's distinctive, systematic way of understanding sociality and *recollection* is his distinctive new conception of an essentially historical form of rationality. Understanding the interrelations between them makes it possible to reconcile the acknowledgment of a central and essential representational dimension to discursive norms with the need for norms to be legitimated by engagement in critical practices of assessment of the rational credentials of claims to authority. It does that by underwriting a recognitive, recollective, *expressive* account of representation that directly responds to Rorty's skepticism about the intelligibility of a nonauthoritarian conception of representational norms.

II

Hegel takes over from Kant the insight that what distinguishes us sapient, discursive beings from merely natural ones is the *normative* character of the space in which we live, and move, and have our being. *Geist*, Hegel's focal concept—what the *Phänomenologie des Geistes* is a phenomenology of—is the whole comprising all of our implicitly norm-governed performances, practices, and institutions, the explicit theoretical expressions of them that constitute our normative self-consciousness, and everything that those normative practices and institutions make possible. The most obvious consequence of treating *Geist* as of co-equal significance with the individual self-consciousnesses who are made what they are by *Geist* and who actualize and reflect on it, is both to *socialize* and then to *historicize* the conception of normativity. For Hegel, *normative* statuses are essentially *social* statuses: products of individuals' practical recognitive attitudes toward one another, aspects of the roles they play in social practices. He is the original social pragmatist about normativity—as Dewey and Rorty acknowledge (though the later Wittgenstein, for instance, does not—much as his thought is also principally animated by this insight).

Hegel also understands us, as normative beings, as essentially *historical* beings—as the kind of thing that has a *history* rather than a *nature*. Thereon hangs a tale. At the base of Hegel's conception of us is the distinction between what we are *in* ourselves and what we are *for* ourselves. We are what things can be something *for*, which is to say that we are *conscious* beings. Hegel understands the origins of this capacity to lie in our nature as organic, desiring beings. A biological desire such as hunger comes with an associated activity that it elicits, in the case of hunger: eating. And it comes with a practical significance the desiring organism can take or treat things as having, by responding to them with that activity: in this example, food. But something that is responded to as food, namely by being eaten, might or might not show itself actually to be food by satisfying the hunger, the desire that motivated the activity. That means that desires institute a distinction between what things are *for* the desiring creature and what they are *in* themselves (how they appear and how they really are). For something is food *for* the hungry animal who eats it, but is actually food, the organism is right practically to assign it that significance, only if it in fact satisfies the hunger. Hegel takes this possibility of practically experiencing *error*, finding out that what was food *for* the hungry organism who ate it was not really—in his idiom "in itself"— food, to be the organic origin of consciousness.[2]

Among the things that can be something *for* conscious beings is those beings themselves. One of the practical significances things can have for us, in addition to food, threat, and so on, is the significance of being other desirers: proto-*selves*. Attributing to another that sort of practical significance is the original form of recognition. And when such proto-recognitive attitudes have the right social structure, we can take ourselves to be such selves. That is the origin of *self*-consciousness. (I will further discuss the simultaneous synthesis of communities and self-conscious individual selves by mutual recognition in the next section.)

Hegel thinks we are self-conscious beings in that sense. But we are not only that. We are, further, *essentially* self-conscious beings. That is, what we are *for* ourselves is an essential compo-nent of what we are *in* ourselves. Essentially self-conscious creatures—those for whom what they are *in* themselves depends on what they are *for* themselves—are subjects of a distinctive kind of transformative, self-creative process. For changing what they are *for* themselves changes what they are *in* themselves. As essentially self-conscious, they are consequently essentially *his-torical* beings. In the place of *natures*, they have *histories*. For if you want to understand what they are in themselves (statuses), you must rehearse the cascade of changes in what they were for themselves (attitudes), which occasioned changes in what they

---

[2] I discuss the rootedness of consciousness in desire and the "tripartite orectic structure of awareness" in the *Phenomenology* in chapter 8 of *A Spirit of Trust*.

were in themselves, followed by new changes in what they were for themselves, and so on.

Things that have histories must be understood in ways that are fundamentally different from the ways things that have natures can be understood. This is the basis of the distinction between the *Geisteswissenschaften* and the *Naturwissenschaften*. Hegel calls the distinctive kind of rational process by which it is possible to understand essentially historical things "recollection" (*Erinnerung*)—a sort of retrospective rational reconstruction of a historical process of development. Because the social recognitive process of instituting norms is also a historical process, Hegel understands normativity, *Geist* itself, as having a history. According to his recollective rational reconstruction, his "phenomenology" of *Geist*, the defining, transformative event in that history—the single most important thing that ever happened to us—is the rolling, extended, still incomplete transition from *traditional* to distinctively *modern* forms of normativity (and so, of selves, their self-consciousness, and their recognitive communities). To understand his conception of this titanic sea-change in the most fundamental metaphysical structure of normativity, we need to look more closely at the vocabulary he deploys to talk about norms—that is, according to Kant's guiding idea, about what makes us *us*, and not just part of *it*.

I understand Hegel's talk about what we are *in* ourselves as talk about our normative *statuses*, and his talk about what we are *for* ourselves as talk about our normative *attitudes*. Each of these is further subdivided. The principal dimensions of what we are *in* ourselves are *independence* and *dependence*. I understand these Hegelian terms, when applied to individual self-conscious selves as normative subjects, to be ways of talking about *authority* and *responsibility* (right and duty, permission and obligation, entitlement and commitment).[3] The principal dimensions of what we are *for* ourselves is what a self-consciousness is for *others* and what it is for *itself*. I understand these to correspond to attitudes of *attribution* to others of normative statuses and attitudes of *acknowledging* or undertaking those statuses ourselves.

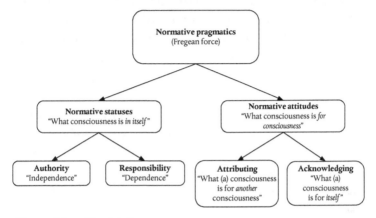

Elements of the model are in bold.
Modeled Hegelian phrases are in quotes.

Put in these terms, what shatters the traditional normative order is the dawning practical and theoretical realization that we *are* essentially self-conscious beings, in the sense that what we are *in* ourselves, our normative statuses, depends on (is responsible to) what we collectively are *for* ourselves, our normative attitudes. It is the discovery of the *attitude-dependence* of *normative statuses*. The contrasting traditional practical understanding, which forms the dark background against which the modern insight stands out in bright relief, sees normative statuses of

---

[3] I do not claim that there are no important differences among these pairs. I take Hegel's "*unabhängig*" and "*abhängig*" to be generic, comprising these pairs as species and marking what they have in common.

authority in the form of *superiority*, and *responsibility* in the form of *subordination*, as objective, attitude-independent features of a normative order we *find* rather than *make*. The purest theoretical expression of this traditional practical conception of norms is the *scala naturae*, the Great Chain of Being. Although it has many dimensions, at its core it is a *normative* order of superiority and subordination: the authority to command and the obligation to obey. At its summit is God, below him all the serried ranks of angels (seraphim, cherubim, thrones, and dominations...all the way down to mere archangels) through the feudal order of kings and lords down to peasants, hierarchically organized animals, vegetables, and minerals (which are apparently fair game to be bossed around by just about everybody—sullen, stubborn, and recalcitrant servants though they might be). Our *cognitive* task is to discover what is fitting or proper (how things objectively ought to be, who has rightful dominion over whom) and our *practical* task is to bring our conduct and subjective *attitudes* into accord with those attitude-independent, objective normative facts (the ought-to-do's determined by "my station and its duties," which articulate the ought-to-be's). The principle organizing this traditional order is accordingly the *status-dependence* of *normative attitudes*. The normative order is traditionally understood as objective (whether natural or supernatural), not the product of subjective attitudes or social practices. It is found and not made.

Hegel understands the practical realization that is the driving motor of modernity as finding explicit expression in the Enlightenment's rejection of this picture as *fetishism*: the projection of the products of the activity of human subjects into an objective form in which they are no longer recognizable as such. Modernity is the replacement of the practical construal of norms structured by implicit commitment to the status-dependence of normative attitudes by a practical and theoretical construal of norms structured by explicit commitment to the attitude-dependence of normative statuses. It is the most important event in the history of *Geist* (so far!). As I am characterizing Hegel's thought, his idea is that social pragmatism about norms is the master idea of modernity, and the Enlightenment is the explicit theoretical self-consciousness of this change of practical attitude. Rorty, Dewey, and Hegel are at one on this point, different as their expressions of it might seem.

Rorty also enthusiastically endorses Hegel's appreciation of the historical mutability of the discursive norms that we now, as moderns, understand as being instituted by the social practices of concept users. As I said at the opening of the first lecture, he saw Hegel as initiating a wholly progressive understanding of us that was socialized and historicized, so broadly naturalized and thoroughly detranscendentalized—a movement culminating in what he himself made of Dewey's pragmatism. My overall contention here is that because Rorty's grasp of the social and historical articulation of normativity that Hegel discovers remains at a highly abstract and programmatic level, he does not understand how the more detailed structure Hegel discerns provides the resources to respond to Rorty's anti-authoritarian critique of the ultimate intelligibility of representational norms. The rational criticizability of normative statuses can be seen to be built into them when we appreciate the social and historical fine structure of the process by which they are instituted by normative attitudes. This is the structure of reciprocal recognition, along the social dimension, and the structure of retrospective recollection, along the historical dimension. Seeing how these interdigitate, and just how the recollective historical balancing of authority and responsibility is a special form of the social recognitive reciprocity of authority and responsibility, is the key to understanding

Hegel's expressive account of the *representational* dimension of conceptual content, and how it satisfies the constraints operative in Rorty's final anti-authoritarian argument for global anti-representationalism. To begin to explicate that thought, I now turn to examine first the social recognitive and then the historical recollective aspects of Hegel's account of the institution of normative statuses by normative attitudes.

III

So far I have indicated how commitment to social pragmatism about normativity is built deeply into Hegel's understanding of the advance modernity makes over traditional ways of under-standing ourselves. It shows up as the realization of the attitude-dependence of normative statuses. In fact it takes the specific form of the idea that normative statuses are *instituted by* practical normative attitudes. The Enlightenment sees, as traditional thin-kers had not, that there were no superiors and subordinates, no authority and responsibility, until people started practically *tak-ing* or *treating* each other *as* superiors and subordinates, author-itative and responsible. It is playing that role in a social web of *practical attitudes* that confers normative significance on the per-formances of participants in social practices of attributing and acknowledging authority and responsibility. That is one of the three commitments I claimed Rorty's skeptical conclusions about representation and represented reality rest on. (The others are a normative understanding of *representation* in terms of authority and responsibility and the idea that genuine authority involves a correlative critical rational responsibility to be responsive to demands for reasons.) Looking at some of the fine structure of Hegel's account of the social practices that institute normative statuses will both show how he subscribes also to the interdependence of authority and rational responsibility Rorty invokes as a second premise, and illuminate the interplay of normative attitudes and normative statuses that is articulated along the historical dimension of Hegel's story.

Kant, too, endorses a version of the modern insight into the attitude-dependence of normative statuses. His normative conception of discursive creatures as *autonomous* is the idea that we are genuinely *normatively* bound only by commitments that we ourselves endorse and acknowledge. This contrasts with merely natural beings, which are bound by laws (norms) that are independent of their attitudes. We are bound rather by our *conceptions* of rules. Only *we* can normatively bind ourselves, by our attitudes. These are the two sides of *autonomy*: νόμος (nomos) and αὐτός (autos), the law and the self-binding by which it becomes efficacious. As I said in the first lecture, this is what Kant makes of Rousseau's dictum that "Obedience to a law one has prescribed to oneself is freedom."[4] The basic Kantian normative status, the status of being an autonomous subject of normative attitudes and statuses, is having the authority to undertake commitments: the authority to *make* oneself responsible by *taking* oneself to be responsible. This is the authority (a normative status) to institute commitments or responsibilities (another kind of status) by adopting an *attitude*: acknowledging or undertaking that commitment or responsibility.[5]

---

[4] "[L]'obéissance à la loi qu'on s'est prescrite est liberté." *Social Contract*, I, viii.

[5] Kant does, of course, acknowledge commitments whose bindingness is *not* up to us in this sense. But these are *categorial* commitments (both theoretical and practical), in the sense of commitments that are implicit in adopting any discursive attitudes at all. These are optional and attitude-dependent only in a thin and very different sense. As Sellars says: "Of course, one could simply not speak—but only at the cost of having nothing to say."

Building on and developing this Kantian idea, Hegel understands normative statuses to be *socially* synthesized by attitudes of what he calls "recognition" (*Anerkennung*), when those recognitive attitudes are reciprocated. Recognizing others is taking them to be normative subjects. That is taking them to be subjects of normative statuses and attitudes: able to be responsible and to exercise authority, and both to attribute those statuses to others and to acknowledge, undertake, or claim them themselves. The intuition at the root of Hegel's socializing of Kant's picture is the idea that genuinely to *be* responsible depends not only on one's *acknowledging* a responsibility oneself, but also on others *holding* one responsible. The institution of normative statuses depends not only on the subject's own attitudes, but also on the attitudes of others, the recognition of those the subject recognizes (attributes that authority).

Kant expresses a weaker version of this idea in his claim that autonomous beings have an obligation to *respect* the autonomy of others. To respect the dignity of others as free beings in this normative sense is to attribute to them the authority to commit themselves, to *make* themselves responsible by *taking* themselves to be responsible. But for Kant, the normative status of autonomy and its dignity is just a fact (albeit a distinctive and distinctively significant kind of fact). And the attitude of respect or recognition by others is merely an appropriate reflection and acknowledgment of it: a status-dependent attitude. Hegel's radical idea is that that attitude of respect or recognition by others is as constitutive of the status as the subject's own commitment-instituting attitudes are. Not only are commitments or responsibilities attitude-dependent statuses, but so is the authority to institute statuses by one's attitudes. Only the right social constellation of attitudes of attributing and acknowledging authority and responsibility institutes genuine normative statuses: actualizing what otherwise remain merely virtual objects of attitudes.

Taking normative statuses to be instituted by reciprocal recognitive attitudes involves assigning to the members of a recognitive community authority and responsibility that are co-ordinate and complementary. It is entirely up to me whom I recognize, in the sense of granting or attributing to them the authority to hold me responsible. But it is neither then up to me whether they recognize me in turn, nor for what exactly they hold me responsible, nor whether they take me to have fulfilled that responsibility. The idea is that what I am actually committed to (this aspect of what I as a normative subject am "in myself," my statuses) is the product both of *my* attitudes and of the attitudes of *others*, whom I recognize and who recognize me—the responsibilities I acknowledge, and what I am held responsible for.

Consider the status of being a good chess player. Achieving that status is not something I can do simply by coming subjectively to adopt a certain attitude toward myself. It is, in a certain sense, up to me whom I regard as good chess players: whether I count any woodpusher who can play a legal game, only formidable club players, only Masters, or even only Grand Masters. That is, it is up to me whom I recognize as good chess players, in the sense in which I aspire to be one. But it is *not* then in the same sense up to me whether I qualify as one of them. To earn their recognition in turn, I must be able to play up to their standards, to earn their recognition. To *be*, say, a formidable club player, I must be recognized as such by those I recognize as such. My recognitive attitudes can define a virtual community, but only the reciprocal recognition by those I recognize can make me actually a member of it, accord me the status for which I have implicitly petitioned by recognizing them. My attitudes exercise recognitive *authority* precisely in determining whose recognitive attitudes I am *responsible* to for my actual normative status.

I can make things hard on myself or easy on myself. I can make it very easy to earn the recognition (in this respect) of those I recognize as good chess players, if I am prepared to set my standards low enough. If I count as a good chess player anyone who can play a legal game, I will not have to learn much in order to earn the recognition by those who can play a legal game of my capacity to play a legal game. The cost is, of course, that what I achieve is only to be entitled to classify myself as a member of this not at all exclusive community. On the other hand, if I want to be entitled to look up to myself (as it were), I can exercise my independence, my authority, and set my standards high, recognizing only Grandmasters as good chess players. To be entitled to class oneself with them, actually to have that status and to be aware of oneself as possessing the status they give concrete determinate content to, would be an accomplishment indeed. But it is not easy to earn their recognition as a good chess player in that sense, that is, by those standards. The thought is that the normative status of being a good writer, or a good philosopher, involves the same sort of constellation of authority and responsibility distributed among members of a community instituted by reciprocal recognitive attitudes.

This story about normative statuses as instituted by reciprocal recognitive attitudes is a sophisticated, richly structured version of social pragmatism about norms. The central application of the reciprocal recognition model of the institution of normative statuses by attitudes is for *discursive* commitments. Language (*Sprache*), Hegel tells us, is the *Dasein* of *Geist*: its concrete, immediate actuality.[6] It is entirely up to me which counter in the

---

[6] Hegel, G.W.F. *Phenomenology of Spirit*, trans. A.V. Miller (Oxford: Oxford University Press, 1977), paragraphs 652 and 666.

language game I play—whether I undertake the commitment expressed by "This coin is copper," for instance. But what exactly I have committed myself to thereby, the content of my commitment, is not up to me. That content is administered by those I (and other users of the term "copper") acknowledge as authoritative, those we recognize as metallurgical experts. They will hold me responsible for being committed to the coin's melting at 1085°C, and to its conducting electricity, even if I have no beliefs, or different beliefs, about copper's melting point and electrical conductivity.

So Hegel also builds deep into his social, reciprocal recognition model of the attitude-dependence of normative statuses (his version of social pragmatism about norms) the reciprocity of authority and responsibility that leads Rorty to be skeptical about the very idea of a nonhuman authority—whether *God*, authoritative over our practical attitudes and commitments, or a represented objective *Reality*, authoritative over our cognitive attitudes and commitments. Recognitive practical normative *attitudes* institute the most basic normative *statuses*: being the subject of normative statuses and attitudes. They do so only when they have the right *social* structure: when they are mutual or reciprocal, which is to say when the *authority* of each member of the recognitive community instituted by those attitudes is balanced by *responsibility* to others, whose recognitive authority has been recognized in turn. Reciprocal recognitive attitudes are normative relations among *us*, because they define who *we* are. We cannot stand in such relations to what is *other*—what is merely "it"—in the sense defined by its contrasting otherness to *us* subjects of normative statuses and attitudes. If there are other significant normative relations that are not themselves recognitive relations, they must be understood ultimately in terms of recognitive attitudes and the normative statuses those attitudes institute. For without reciprocal recognition, there is no normativity, no *Geist*. This is all fully in accord with Rorty's account and the motivations for it. Hegel just has—not surprisingly—a more detailed constructive, systematic story about the metaphysics of normativity: about the recognitive fine structure of norm-instituting social practices. Rorty, like his hero Wittgenstein and his fellow Wittgensteinian McDowell, is not disposed to think philosophers should so much as aspire to tell such stories. But I think we have here an index example of the kind of substantive philosophical understanding such principled theoretical quietism spurns.

Hegel also takes over from Kant a normative understanding of the significance of specifically representational relations. They agree that however they are established or instituted, to count as *representational* relations, whatever plays the role of represent*eds* must exercise a distinctive kind of *authority over* what can only count as represent*ings* of them if they are suitably *responsible to* those representeds. What is represented must be intelligible as providing a normative standard authoritative for assessments of the correctness of representings of it, in a distinctive (representational) sense of "correctness." Liability to *attitudes* that are assessments of correctness set by what thereby counts as represent*ed* is constitutive of having the normative *status* of a represent*ing*. In such assessments of the correctness of representings as representings we see one locus where *critical* rational practices get a grip.

The issues that worry Rorty are reflected in Hegel's more articulated and systematic social pragmatism about norms by the fact these normative relations of representational authority and responsibility are not symmetric and reciprocal in the way they would have to be to be immediately intelligible on the model of reciprocal recognition. The authority of representeds over representings and the responsibility of representings to them are complementary only in the trivial sense that if X has authority over Y, Y is responsible to X (and *vice versa*). Recognitive reciprocity requires in addition that if X has authority over Y (Y is responsible to X) then Y has authority over X (X is responsible to Y). Each interlocutor X has the authority to recognize any Y, but that is the authority to grant to Y a corresponding authority: the authority to hold X responsible. In the representational case, the authority of representeds over representings (the responsibility of representings to representeds) is not balanced by a symmetric authority of representings over representeds (responsibility of representeds to representings). The idea that there is such a reciprocal authority of representings over representeds is a kind of subjective idealism that is as foreign to Hegel as it is to Rorty.

So as I read him, Hegel endorses all three of the premises of Rorty's anti-authoritarian, global anti-representationalist argument for the conclusion that we should reject as fetishistic the idea of the ultimate authority of a represented nonhuman, natural objective reality over our *cognitive* practices—as and for the same reasons that we reject as fetishistic the idea of the ultimate authority of a nonhuman, supernatural being over our *ethical* practices:

- Both have ground-level commitments to social pragmatism about normativity: the idea that norms and normative significances are instituted by playing roles in our social practices, and the constellations of practical attitudes they make possible.
- Further, Hegel's particular model of the social institution of normative statuses by reciprocal recognitive attitudes builds in Rorty's insight that part of what the Enlightenment was

rejecting about traditional understandings of normativity was the idea of *authority* not balanced by complementary *responsibility*. Genuine authority must be *rational* authority, in the sense that we are obliged to acknowledge the authority only of what we are in a position to hold responsible for providing *reasons* for its exercises of that authority.

- Finally, Rorty and Hegel agree with the Kantian analysis of representational relations as fundamentally normative relations of authority and responsibility between representeds and representings.

Rorty argues that if we think through the implications of these first two ideas, we will see as confused and ultimately unintelligible the idea that the meaningfulness of our discourse is constituted by, or even essentially dependent on, normative representational relations between things that *can* give and ask for reasons and things that *cannot* participate in those reasoning practices, cannot adopt those attitudes. We should not acknowledge the *authority* of what we cannot interrogate and hold *responsible* for its reasons. In spite of their many fundamental agreements in this vicinity, however, Hegel does *not* follow Rorty in rejecting the idea of a normatively inflected, specifically *representational* dimension to the contents of our discursive commitments. Nor does he reject the idea of an objective reality exercising authority over our cognitive commitments that that representational dimension of conceptual contentfulness underwrites. So the question I want to address is: How can Hegel reconcile that with his embrace of the modern insight into the attitude-dependence of normative statuses, and his understanding of the institution of normative statuses by reciprocal recognitive attitudes?

IV

Hegel takes modernity's discovery of the attitude-dependence of normative statuses, which is social pragmatism about normativity, to be a decisive advance in our (and so *Geist's*) self-consciousness. We have come to understand that our practical attitudes play an essential role in instituting the norms, governance by which makes us discursive, sapient, essentially self-conscious, historical beings, and not merely natural desiring ones. But he also thinks that this self-understanding is partial and incomplete, and that the evident substantial gain is mixed with a complementary loss. There is a worm in the apple of modernity. He calls it "alienation" (*Entfremdung*). Alienation in his usage is not a psychological matter (though it has psychological effects). It is a defect in the metaphysical structure of modern normativity. In grossest terms it is a loss of the *binding force* of the norms. He calls what is lost "*Sittlichkeit*," after *Sitte*, customs or mores, the traditional implicit form of governing norms.

While Hegel whole-heartedly applauds the overcoming of the fetishism that takes norms to be objective features of the non-human world, something merely there, antecedently to and independently of our attitudes toward them, he thinks that coming to see them explicitly as products of our practices—as something *we* are *responsible* for—threatens to undercut their practical rational *authority* over us. Hegel thinks that traditional commitment to the status-dependence of normative attitudes expressed a genuine insight, even though that insight took the deformed shape of the fetishistic reification of norms. Practical attitudes are intelligible as genuinely *normative* attitudes only if they are answerable or responsible to, governed by, the norms (the statuses) they are attitudes toward—the authority and responsibility they attribute or acknowledge.

The authority of norms over attitudes—the sense in which practical attitudes and conduct are bound or governed by norms—is two-fold. It has deontic and alethic dimensions. First, the norms serve as *standards for normative assessments* of the correctness or propriety of attitudes. One *should attribute* to others or *acknowledge* oneself what the parties are actually committed to, the authority or responsibility that they really have. What they are for us should be what they are in themselves. That is something one can get wrong. Second, the attitudes one adopts should be *subjunctively sensitive* to the contents of the statuses acknowledged or attributed, in the sense that if the norms or statuses *were* or *had been* different, the acknowledgments and attributions *would be* or *would have been* different. These are the two dimensions along which norms are practically efficacious as making a difference to the attitudes, and so to the conduct of participants in the practice. Having this sort of significance is essential to its being genuinely *normative* statuses that are being acknowledged and attributed, toward which attitudes are being adopted.

Hegel thinks there is a substantial tension between norm-governedness in this sense and the modern appreciation of the attitude-dependence of norms. Seeing the norms as products of our attitudes can make it impossible to see those attitudes as genuinely governed by the resulting norms, in this dual sense. As Wittgenstein puts his version of the point: "One would like to say: whatever is going to seem right to me is right. And that only means that here we can't talk about 'right.'"[7] Alienation is losing

---

[7] *Philosophical Investigations*, trans. G.E.M. Anscombe (New York, Macmillan, 1953), §258.

our grip on the intelligibility of norms as genuinely *binding* on us, as a result of understanding them as instituted by our own attitudes. The result is a picture that is attitudes "all the way down," unanchored in actual norms. (Notice that where the issue is alienation from the normative products of our own attitudes, it is no use to invoke the *social* dimension of the institution of normative statuses by recognitive attitudes so as to try to understand *my* attitudes as bound by the norms instituted by *our* attitudes. For the question is how *our* attitudes can be so bound.)

Alienation in this sense is pretty much what Rorty's *pragmatism* both endorses in theory and adopts in practice. Rorty deliberately chooses the Romantic and Hegelian term "irony" for the sort of private detachment from the commitments that govern our public life that he recommends and esteems.[8] Rorty is well aware that in his discussion of alienation in the *Spirit* chapter of the *Phenomenology*, Hegel identifies Romantic irony as one of the most characteristic expressions of alienated modernity. Hegel would see Rorty's version of Deweyan pragmatism as a clear-eyed acknowledgment and deliberate embracing of our modern, alienated predicament. As according to Kant I am genuinely *normatively* bound only by norms whose bindingness I acknowledge (explicitly or implicitly), so for Rorty we are bound only by those norms we can agree on. To have real authority or responsibility just *is* to be practically taken or treated *as* authoritative or held responsible by the community. (That is the serious thought behind such characteristic Rortyan throw-away lines as "The truth is whatever your community will let you get away with.") There is not, and cannot intelligibly be,

---

[8] *Locus classicus* is, of course, his 1989 book *Contingency, Irony, and Solidarity* (Cambridge: Cambridge University Press, 1989).

anything *else* that is authoritative over our practices and practical attitudes. That is the form Rorty's anti-authoritarianism takes.

It is a consequence he draws from his social pragmatism about norms. He agrees with Hegel in seeing the idea that our social practices institute the norms we are bound by as the principal lesson of the original Enlightenment. Authority as superiority and responsibility as subordination are not statuses ordained by God and revealed in scripture, nor are they natural states to be discerned by careful empirical investigation. (A thought well epitomized both in Shakespeare's line "The fault...is not in the stars, that we are underlings, but in our-selves," and in the rude, traditional but radical, rhetorical ques-tion: "When Adam delved and Eve span, who was then the gentleman?") As we have seen, in calling for the completion of this movement in a second Enlightenment, Rorty appeals to the essentially *normative* character of *representational* relations to assimilate the idea of an objective represented Reality *cognitively* authoritative over our representings of it (theoretical attitudes) to that of God or an objective *scala naturae practically* authoritative over the propriety of our conduct. For him, both fall under the heading of "nonhuman authority over human attitudes," and are accordingly to be rejected.

Hegel disagrees. He thinks what is needed is a postmodern reconciliation of the modern insight into the attitude-dependence of normative statuses with a suitably *un*alienated reappropriation of the traditional *sittlich* insight into the status-dependence of normative attitudes. The aim of such a synthetic reappropriation is to re-establish the intelligibility of the bindingness—the *rational* bindingness, the genuine authority—of norms that, though instituted by our practical attitudes, nonetheless transcend those attitudes sufficiently to normatively govern them (both deontically as standards of assessment and alethically in terms of subjunctive sensitivity). Among the various kinds of attitude-transcendent norms he countenances, Hegel treats as central and essential those that articulate the representational dimension of conceptual content: the authority of represented states of affairs over representings of them in thought and talk. By contrast to Rorty, he thinks that the relations between representeds and representings are intelligible as normative relations of authority and responsibility even though we do not recognize what exercises representational authority as one of us givers-of and askers-for reasons.

In particular, to be accorded normative authority by our critically rational practices and attitudes, what is represented need *not* itself, for Hegel, either be recognized by us as the subject of normative recognitive attitudes, nor itself adopt such recognitive attitudes toward us. Having our attitudes normatively governed (in the dual sense) by something that does not itself have normative attitudes—and so cannot and is not obliged to give reasons for such attitudes—is not, Hegel claims, incompatible with the modern insight that normative statuses are instituted by normative attitudes. What is required is only that the normative statuses of authority and responsibility constitutive of the representational relation between representeds and representings be *instituted* by our attitudes toward them, by the role they play in our practices. The challenge he faces in making out this claim in a way compatible with the insights and commitments he shares with Rorty is to say just how we need to act, what we need to *do*, so as to *confer* distinctively *representational* normative significance on what thereby acquire the practical normative significance both of representeds and representings—and how the significances so conferred make representational norms subject to critical rational appraisal.

V

The general form of Hegel's strategy for overcoming alienation and reachieving *Sittlichkeit*, by reconciling the modern insight into the attitude-dependence of normative statuses with the traditional insight into the status-dependence of normative attitudes, is to appeal to the *historical* structure of the constellation of reciprocal authority and responsibility that relates attitudes and statuses. He understands *past* attitudes as having instituted the norms that govern our current and future attitudes. The engine of his account is the idea of a new sort of rational activity: *recollection* (*Erinnerung*). It is possible that only someone who, like Hegel, was writing as part of the generation that invented intellectual history in the modern sense could have come up with this idea (though of course it has roots that reach further back, for instance in Herder and Vico).

Recollection is a retrospective rational reconstruction that selects and assembles from the series of attitudes that have actually been adopted by practitioners an *expressively progressive* trajectory through them. To say that it is expressively progressive is to say that the reconstructed path has the shape of the gradual emergence into explicitness of a norm that can with hindsight be seen to have implicitly governed the process all along. Recollection turns a mere *past* into a *history*: the past comprehended as normatively significant.[9] Recollection confers normative significance on the sequence of past attitudes

[9] Hegel here develops Herder's idea: "The mere narrator is an annalist, a writer of memoirs, of newspapers; the reasoner about the individual narration is a historical rationalizer; but the man who orders many occurrences into a plan, into a vision—he is … the true historical artist … he is the creator of a *history*." Johann Gottfried Herder, "Older Critical Forestlets," In *Herder:*

(applications of concepts) by exhibiting it as having the distinctive norm-instituting recognitive structure of a *tradition*. That is a quite specific constellation of authority of the past over the present and future, and authority of the present and future over the past. It is a kind of active *making* (institution of norms) that has the form of a *finding* of a norm as already governing the prior attitudes. The content of the norm is recollected as constant throughout, with each included episode of applying the norm by adopting an attitude serving to reveal a bit more of that content, further expressing it by making explicit aspects that had hitherto remained implicit.

A helpful model is provided by the evolution of legal concepts in Anglo-American common law.[10] Here there is no initial explicit governing statute. *All* there is to determine the content of the legal concepts being applied is the history of their prior application by earlier judges. For this reason it is sometimes described as "judge-made law." (Even where there is an explicit statute, case law articulating it develops in the same way as common law.) The *only* authority a judge can claim for her decision to apply or withhold the application to a new set of facts of a concept of common law (such as *negligence* or *strict liability*) is the authority of earlier decisions. The rationale or justification for such a decision takes the form of a recollection of prior judicial attitudes, as expressed in those decisions. From the welter of the actual record, some decisions are retrospectively privileged by being treated as precedential, as having a

Philosophical Writings, edited by Michael N. Forster (Cambridge: Cambridge University Press, 2002), p. 260.

[10] I explore this jurisprudential model further in "A Hegelian Model of Legal Concept Determination: The Normative Fine Structure of the Judges' Chain Novel," In *Pragmatism, Law, and Language*, edited by Graham Hubbs and Douglas Lind (New York: Routledge, 2014), pp. 19–39.

certain kind of authority over future applications of those legal concepts. They are treated as having gradually but inexorably revealed important contours of the content of the concept in question. A tradition is reconstructed, consisting entirely of episodes treated as precedential, and hence authoritative as to the content of the norm being discerned. In order properly to rationalize and justify the current decision, that tradition must be presented as the cumulative, progressive clarification of a norm (law) made visible as operative throughout the process. The reasons the judge gives for her current decision take the form of an explicit codification of the lessons learned along the way, as different aspects of the implicit norm or concept are shown as being brought into the explicit light of day by precedential decisions. (The inevitable cases where this cannot be done must be decided on grounds other than *stare decesis*—since they must be decided. But treating a case as wholly novel in this sense, as one of "first impression," is always a last resort and a confession of a certain kind of failure. The failure is the inability to ground the authority of the new decision in its responsibility to and acknowledgment of the authority of precedent.)

In common and case law, there is no content to the norm except what it has been imbued with by the authority of such jurisprudential decisions. That authority is *rational* authority in the sense that prior decisions provide *reasons* capable of justifying future decisions. That authority in each case essentially involves a correlative rational responsibility, however. That responsibility to provide reasons, to offer a rationale (by appeal to prior decisions) is administered by future judges. For they will recognize the precedential authority of the current decision only insofar as they take it to be licensed or rationalized by, responsible to, a suitable acknowledgment of the authority of the prior decisions privileged as precedential by those future judges in *their* recollective vindications of their own decisions. The authority of each decision depends on the *reasons* for it that can recollectively be extracted from the rationally reconstructed tradition it discerns. *Recollection* is accordingly a distinctive kind of critical *rationalization*. It is a process of rationalization that both *produces* and acknowledges reasons, a process, as Hegel puts it, both of giving *contingency* the (normative) form of *necessity* and of acknowledging the necessitating (normative) force of reasons.

Though historical recollective developmental processes are essentially *a*symmetrical, insofar as they are diachronic (later judges cannot demand responses from earlier ones), they also exhibit the *symmetrical* structure of authority and responsibility characteristic of reciprocal recognition. Each judge is both a recognizer and a petitioner for recognition—recognition that, if successful, results in the judge being recognized in turn. The judge only has the normative status she claims, the reason-instituting authority of a correct or even precedential decision, if she is in fact recognized as having it by future judges, who adopt attitudes of attributing that authority. The ones she recognizes (the prior judges to whom she attributes precedential authority, to whom she accordingly acknowledges responsibility) are not the same individuals on whose recognition she depends for the actualization of her attitudes, for the transformation of her claim to reason-instituting authority into the actual status of such authority. Those are the future judges, who assess the fidelity of her recollection to the authority of reason-giving precedents to which they themselves acknowledge rational responsibility. Yet she, like all the rest of the judges in the tradition, has authority only insofar as she succeeds in making herself responsible to the attitudes of others in the diachronic recognitive community, that is, the tradition, constituted by their recollections. She makes herself recognitively *responsible* to both past and future judges in these different but symmetrical ways, by adopting the attitude of claiming *authority* that is implicit in making a decision at all.

It is of the essence of recollection that the concepts, norms, or laws that emerge from this process (that jurisprudential recollection reveals and makes more explicit) can *both* be "judge-made" *and* provide genuine *reasons* for deciding cases one way rather than another. The deciding judge recollectively claims the *authority* of what she takes or treats as precedent, as providing reasons for her decision. Those reasons, and the norms they articulate, are genuine, actually have the authority claimed for them, just insofar as they are recognized in turn *as* reasons, as normatively binding, by later judges, who have the authority to treat the present decision as itself precedential and authoritative, insofar as it is taken suitably to have fulfilled its *responsibility* to the reasons provided by the tradition it both inherits and retrospectively constitutes. The norm-instituting, norm-acknowledging recognitive process that consists of recollective rational reconstruction of a tradition and recollective reconstruction of prior recollections is the form Hegel presents as paradigmatically *critical*. For in it claims to rational authority are perfectly balanced by the responsibility to give reasons justifying such claims. In this paradigmatically historical process, any stable equilibrium is fragile and temporary, but no claimed authority is beyond rational assessment and criticism as to its rational credentials.

Hegel thinks that the recollective-recognitive process that I have described as determining the content of *legal* concepts in common law jurisprudence also determines the contents of our ordinary *empirical* descriptive concepts, and that of their sophisticated scientific relatives. In the case of applying empirical concepts, as opposed to legal ones, he understands each phase of the process of experience (*Erfahrung*, by contrast to the episodic, self-intimating episodes of *Erlebnis*) to include three stages. It begins with the *registration* of an anomaly: the acknowledgment that one finds oneself with commitments that are *incompatible*, by one's own lights, according to one's own understanding of the contents to which one is committed. They are incompatible in the sense that one cannot become entitled to them both (or to all of them). Because the motor of experience is always the acknowledgment of the conflict of one's commitments with each other, for Hegel experience is always the experience of *error*. Practically acknowledging that material incompatibility is taking oneself to be obliged to *do* something, *change* something. This is the obligation to engage in a process of *repair* of the anomaly, to replace rational discord with rational harmony, by altering or giving up some of the offending commitments.

This much is already in Kant, as Hegel reads him. What one is doing in making a judgment is undertaking a specific task-responsibility: the responsibility to *do* something. What one is undertaking the responsibility to do is to rationally integrate that commitment with one's prior commitments, by finding reasons justifying it, acknowledging the consequences that follow from it, and (the case that matters most for Hegel) resolving any incompatibilities that result from taking the new claim on board. Doing this is what Kant calls "synthesizing" a constellation of commitments that exhibits the sort of systematic rational unity distinctive of sapient awareness: the "synthetic unity of apperception." At this point, though, Hegel moves decisively beyond the Kantian paradigm, by adding a crucial further constraint on what counts as successful repairs of commitments acknowledged as discordant.

When anomalies occur, perhaps prompted by perceptual judgments noninferentially wrenched from the subject as the immediate deliverances of sense (the passive exercises of conceptual abilities), not just any rejiggering that removes the incompatibility suffices. Successful repairs must *explain* and *justify* the changes made, in a special way, by taking a distinctive form. Vindication of a proposed reparative strategy in response to an acknowledgment of incompatible commitments must take the form of a special kind of *historical* narrative: a recollection. One must tell a retrospective story that rationally reconstructs an idealized expressively progressive trajectory through previous changes of view that culminates in the view being endorsed after the repair of the most recently discovered anomaly. In the first stage of the experience of error, the previous conception of how things are, what played the role *to* consciousness of what things are *in* themselves, has been unmasked as appearance, and has accordingly shifted status. It now plays the role *to* consciousness of being only what things were *for* consciousness: an erroneous view of how things really are. The idea is that to justify endorsing a new view as veridically representing how thing really are, in themselves, one must show how, assuming that things are that way, one did or could have come to *know* that things are that way. This is fulfilling one's critical rational responsibility to exhibit *reasons* for the commitment one is undertaking—a necessary condition of its having the authority it claims.

Doxastically endorsing a conceptual content is taking it to be fact-stating: to present how things are in themselves. That *what* one takes to be facts (which contents, exactly, one endorses) *changes* over time is just a change in status of the contents involved during the registration and repair stages of the experience of error. The old content changes status from being endorsed to not being endorsed, and its replacement changes status from not being endorsed to being endorsed. What was *to* consciousness noumenal *reality* is unmasked as phenomenal *appearance*, and replaced by a different content, newly endorsed as objectively factual. The recollective stage of an experience of error justifies this change of status by forging a distinctive kind of link between the content newly endorsed as noumenal and all the previously endorsed contents that now are taken to be phenomena. And here we come to the crux. It is a *representational* link, in virtue of which they show up to the conscious subject as phenomenal appearances *of* that noumenal reality. The representational link is forged by offering a retrospective recollective rational reconstruction of a sequence of phenomena culminating in the facts as one currently takes them to be. That rational reconstruction exhibits them as all along implicitly normatively governed by their link to that noumenal reality, in the sense that it serves as the normative standard by which their adequacy *as* phenomenal appearances of it is to be assessed and that the attitudes in the expressively progressive recollected trajectory are exhibited as subjunctively sensitive to the represented reality. The same recollective process that finds norms (statuses) governing sequences of actual attitudes is also intelligible as one whereby one finds out what is represented by a sequence of representings.

Doxastic commitments are not just fact-expressing. For Hegel they are, further, implicitly *knowledge* claims. The demand for recollective vindication of one's commitments codifies Hegel's version of the critical justification dimension of claims to knowledge. This distinctive kind of justification requires showing how the previous views one held in the process leading up to the current candidate can properly be understood as views, appearances, or representings *of* what one now endorses as the reality one claims was all along appearing or being represented. To be entitled to claim that things are as one now takes them to be, one must show how one *found out* that they are so. Doing that involves explaining what one's earlier views got right, what they got wrong, and why. It involves rationally reconstructing the sequence of one's previous views of what one now takes to be the same topic so as to exhibit it as a process of *learning*, of gradual *discovery* of how things actually are, of how it is with what one was all along representing (talking or thinking *of* or *about*). This is the progressive emergence into explicitness, the ever more adequate expression, of what is retrospectively discerned as having been all along implicit as the norm governing and guiding (the paired deontic and alethic dimensions) the process by which its appearances arise and pass away. Offering such a retrospective historical rational reconstruction of the process leading up to the constellation of commitments whose endorsement is being vindicated as the lesson properly to be learned from the earlier registering and reparative phases is the final, *recollective* phase of an episode of the experience of error. It essentially involves both the assessment and the offering of reasons.

Recollection transforms a mere description of past commitments into a progressive narrative of a sequence of lessons showing how the way things really are, in themselves (according to one's current commitments), gradually came to be revealed, through that progressive sequence of ever more adequate appearances (what things are or were *for* consciousness), culminating in one's current happy state of (as one takes it to be) *knowledge* of how things really are. A recollecting narrative is a narrative of *expressive* progress. It is a story about how what is now revealed to have been all along *implicit* in prior commitments, as the reality they were appearances of (the noumena behind the phenomena), gradually emerged to become fully *explicit*, showing up as what it really is, in the view currently endorsed, in which that process culminated. It is a story of how what things are *in themselves* ("an sich") becomes what they are *for consciousness*.

> Already something thought, the *content* is the property of substance; existence has no more to be changed into the form of what is in-itself and implicit, but only the *implicit*—no longer merely something primitive, or lying hidden within existence, but already present as a *recollection*—into the form of what is *explicit*, of what is objective to self.
>
> (*Phenomenology of Spirit* paragraph 29)

A recollection accordingly exhibits past commitments that have been discarded because of their incompatibility with others as genuine (if only partially correct) appearances (representings) *of* a represented reality as it is now known to be, and in that sense as not *merely* illusory.

This recollective story about the representational dimension of conceptual content offers an *expressive* account of it. It explains how what was, according to each recollection, always *implicit* ("*an sich*," what things are in themselves), becomes ever more *explicit* (for consciousness). The recollective story is an *expressively* progressive one. The representational relation between senses and referents is established by displaying a sequence of appearances that are ever more adequate expressions of an underlying reality. In general Hegel thinks we can understand what is implicit only in terms of the expressive process by which it is made explicit. That is a recollective process. The underlying reality is construed as implicit in the sense of being a norm that all along governed the process of its gradual emergence into explicitness. Without at any earlier point being fully explicit to the consciousness undergoing the experience, according to the recollection that unveils it as what the appearances were appearances of, that reality nonetheless practically (hence, implicitly) governed the process. According to the retrospective rational reconstruction that is the recollection, it served as a normative standard for better and worse appearances, accordingly as they revealed (expressed) that reality more adequately. And according to the recollection, those assessments were efficacious. The recollective reconstruction exhibits the sequence of ever more adequate appearances as subjunctively sensitive to how things eventually can be seen really to have been, throughout the process of gradually improving representings of it. The meta-norm that governs recollection (determining better and worse recollections) demands *expressive* progress: progress in making explicit what shows up as having been all along implicit. This recollective notion of *expression* is more fundamental than the notion of *representation* it is called on to explain.

Telling that sort of recollective reconstructive story is offering a *phenomenology* of a view (a set of commitments). A phenomenology vindicates that view by showing how it gradually emerged into the explicit light of day from the partial, variously erroneous appearances of it. This is what Hegel does at the metalevel for various "shapes" of self-consciousness (and ultimately, of the whole of *Geist*) in the *Phenomenology*. The final, adequate form of self-consciousness ("Absolute Knowing") knows itself as engaging in a process of this historical recollective kind in its dynamic experience of ground-level empirical and practical commitments and the determinate concepts that articulate them, as well as in its experience of the metaconceptual "shapes" through which it passes. Such a phenomenology vindicates the endorsement of some conceptual contents as noumenal reality, as objectively factual, by showing how they explain the sequential variety of phenomenal appearances by which a subject comes to know them *as* noumenal reality, and thereby explain the advent of that knowledge.

A recollective reconstruction does that by exhibiting the various erroneous beliefs *that* things are thus and so (phenomena) as appearances *of* the facts as they really are (noumena). A recollection performs a great reversal: what eventuates from a process of repeated experiences of error, as its final (thus far) *end* or result, is placed, as it were, also at the *beginning* of the sequence.

> We shall not cease from exploration
> And the end of all our exploring
> Will be to arrive where we started
> And know the place for the first time.[11]

(Hegel often uses circular imagery in this connection.) For the fact is seen as what drives its progressive revelation. How things actually are is recollectively revealed as normatively governing the process both deontically, as a standard of assessment of expressive success, and alethically, as that to which the episodes that count as expressively progressive are subjunctively sensitive. It is at once the cause of a course of experience and its goal. In the case of phenomenological recollection, the conceptual content that is endorsed as factual, as the underlying noumenon, is taken to be *referred to* (represented) by all the phenomena thereby linked to it as appearances (representings) *of* it.

It should be added, though it is not our purpose here to pursue the point, that I have been discussing how things look exclusively from the *retro*spective recollective rationalizing point of view. The very same triphasic process of *registration* of incompatible commitments, *repair* of the incompatibility, and recollective rational *reconstruction* of an expressively progressive

---

[11] T.S. Eliot, "Little Gidding," V, in *Four Quartets* (New York: Harcourt, Brace and Co., 1943).

trajectory through past commitments vindicating the repair looks very different when viewed from a complementary *prospective* temporal perspective. Looking backward, the recollective task is to make visible steady, cumulative progress in revealing how things always already were and are now known to be. Looking forward reveals the ruptures, gaps, contradictions, and mistakes, the ignorance, wrong turns, and failures to understand that inevitably mark the course of conceptual development as having the shape of the experience of *error*. Seen from this point of view, the way to truth is a fallibilist path along which skeptical despair threatens, as every only temporarily stable constellation of commitments dissolves, revealing itself as having been appearance rather than the reality as which it masqueraded. Indeed, Hegel thinks that for reasons of deep metaphysical principle there can be no set of determinate empirical or practical concepts whose *correct* application, according to the norms articulating their contents, will not lead eventually to commitments that are incompatible by their own lights. That is his version of the way in which the immediate (noninferential) deliverances of sense outrun and overflow what is captured conceptually. Kant, like his empiricist predecessors, understood this in terms of its being an infinite task to capture sensuous immediacy conceptually in judgments. There will always be something still not captured. Hegel understands the surplus of the sensuous over the conceptual—immediacy over mediation—rather in terms of the necessary *instability* of any set of empirical concepts: the way their application will show their inadequacy, the need to change them. This shift from understanding the limits of conceptualization in terms of *inexhaustibility* to understanding it in terms of *instability* is of the essence of Hegelian *Vernunft*. The larger point I can only gesture at here is that it is essential to Hegel's view that the sunny Whiggish retrospective progressive and constructive perspective I have been emphasizing and the dark pessimistic prospective perspective of unavoidable error and dissolution be understood as complementary and reciprocally interdependent.

VI

Hegel understands the *social* fine structure of normativity in terms of *communities* ("social substance") synthesized by reciprocal *recognition*. He understands the *historical* fine structure of normativity in terms of *traditions* retrospectively synthesized by *recollection*. Along both dimensions, norms precipitate out of, are instituted by, attitudes. That is the attitude-dependence of normative statuses that is the principal discovery of modernity. But the picture is not attitudes all the way down. Recognitive attitudes do institute genuine normative statuses, and those norms are made visible as genuinely governing attitudes in turn. Practical attitudes or performances are genuinely governed by norms or statuses in the sense I have been discussing only if they are responsible to those norms along two dimensions: deontic and alethic. It is a criterion of adequacy by which recollections are assessed (by future recollectors) that the norms they discern are authoritative for all the attitudes in the retrospectively constituted tradition. They provide standards for assessment of the correctness of those attitudes, which are in that sense genuinely responsible to them. And all the prior attitudes (applications of concepts) that are certified by a recollective rational reconstruction as expressively progressive, as precedential or correct, are exhibited as having been subjunctively sensitive to, and in that sense not only *responsible* to but *responsive* to, the implicit norm of which they explicate some aspect. Normative governance of attitudes in this dual sense of their deontic responsibility and alethic subjunctive sensitivity to norms is the status-dependence of normative attitudes. The result of the rational reconstruction of an expressively progressive tradition by recollection is the revelation of a governing norm to which the attitudes that make up that tradition are both responsible and responsive. That is exactly what is required for something to stand in the normative relation of represented to representings of it.

So Hegel offers an account both of how normative statuses are instituted by reciprocal recognition, and how they become recollectively visible as having genuinely binding force over attitudes. In this way he reconciles the *modern* appreciation of the attitude-dependence of normative statuses with a reconceived version of the *traditional* commitment to the status-dependence of normative attitudes. By doing so, he shows us that alienation from our norms is not an inevitable consequence of the modern insight. That central implicit insight of modernity, we have seen, just is social pragmatism about normativity. Hegel shows how pragmatists need not be normative nihilists— or *merely* ironists. Because the sort of conceptual norms discerned by recollection provide genuine *reasons* for judgments and actions (as in, but not only in courts of law), it also shows that pragmatists need not be irrationalists. Both of these are conclusions Rorty argued for and sought to defend—though not by wheeling in the heavy metaconceptual machinery of recognition and recollection that Hegel deploys.

I suggested earlier that endorsing social pragmatism about normativity—acknowledging that norms are instituted by social practices—need not rule out a community's investing normative significance in something other than themselves. A community can grant authority to the flights of birds or the patterns of fire-induced cracks on a tortoise shell by taking or treating those natural occurrences as normatively significant. That is one form that practical attitudes instituting normative statuses can take. Anthropology provides many examples of just such conferral of normative significance on the natural—as Rorty's friend and Princeton colleague Clifford Geertz would have been the first to remind him. Of course, for Hegel it is characteristic of the premodern practical understanding of such norms to objectify, reify, and so fetishize the resulting norms. It is in these terms that, in his allegorical treatment of Sophocles's *Antigone*, Hegel considers and criticizes the Greeks' treatment of natural differences between biological males and females as *objective* (attitude-independent) markers of different bundles of rights and responsibilities with respect to family and polis. Hegel's account of critical, legitimating recollective rationality gives us the conceptual tools to see in detail how the social investiture of normative significance in natural phenomena provides a way to make pragmatist sense of specifically *representational* cognitive relations to them.

I also considered Rorty's rejoinder to the pointing-out of this possibility. Pragmatists about semantics understand the contents of our utterances and thoughts in terms of the functional role they play in norm-governed discursive social practices. Specifically *discursive* authority and responsibility is essentially, and not just accidentally, *rational* authority and responsibility. And for pragmatists like Rorty, following Dewey—both of them willing to credit Kant with articulating and championing this Enlightenment insight—rationality is unintelligible apart from its *critical* dimension. The authority conferred by reasons is inseparable from the liability speakers and thinkers have to critical demands for *reasons* for the commitments they avow and acknowledge. The authority of their claims is conditional on their legitimating that authority by fulfilling their responsibility to provide suitable reasons for those claims, when appropriately challenged to do so. Kant was right to see the task-responsibility that gives practical weight to cognitive claims—what one must *do* in order to be entitled to the authority one claims—to be the responsibility to vindicate them by offering *reasons justifying* those commitments, and to acknowledge the further commitments for which they provide reasons in turn. (As Locke was right to condition credibility and respect for the testimony of others to the extent to which they apportion their assent to their evidence.[12]) *This* kind of authority, *discursive* authority, the sort of authority that provides *reasons* for us to believe what is claimed, can in principle only be possessed or exercised by those who participate with us in our practices of giving and asking for reasons: persons, not things. It is this thought that grounds the deep connection Rorty, following Dewey, sees between a proper *semantics* and a liberal democratic *politics*: between *reason* and *freedom*. (It is the basis for the philosophical commonality Habermas and Rorty always felt for each other, in spite of the many differences between their views, both about semantics and about politics.)

Hegel, as I have been reading him, agrees both with the observation that social pragmatism is compatible with a community's conferring normative statuses on things that cannot adopt normative attitudes and with the basis of Rorty's skepticism about that idea: Kant's Enlightenment insight that rational authority is inseparable from a correlative critical responsibility to provide reasons. Social practices of giving and asking for

[12] *An Essay Concerning Human Understanding* (Oxford, Clarendon 1959), p. 366. A. Wierzbicka has a fascinating discussion of the cultural resonance and significance of Locke's concern, in chapter 2 of *English: Meaning and Culture* (Oxford: Oxford University Press, 2006).

reasons are necessarily the basis of discursive practice and the norms such practice institutes and applies. But on that basis Hegel then builds a further kind of rationality: historical, recollective rationality. This telling of Hegel's story revolves around two master ideas. First, on the pragmatic side, is a social understanding of normativity in terms of *mutual recognition*. In Hegel's terms, explaining how cognition presupposes recognition is explaining how consciousness presupposes self-consciousness. Kant had justified that characteristically German Idealist claim by appeal to the transcendental unity of apperception. For Hegel, as for his pragmatist successors, all transcendental constitution is social institution (as my former colleague John Haugeland liked to put the point). Second, articulating Hegel's pragmatism, is the conception of a new kind of rationality. It consists in a historical understanding of the relations between conceptual content and implicitly normative discursive practices in terms of an *expressive* process of *recollection*. Each of these ideas comprises a number of subsidiary ones, and is articulated by an intricate fine structure relating them.

The model of expression as recollection—the story about what one must *do* to count as thereby making explicit something that was implicit—is in many ways the keystone of the edifice. It explains the representational semantic and cognitive relation between how things appear "for consciousness" on the *subjective* side of *thought* and how things really are "in themselves" on the *objective* side of *being*: the relation between appearance and reality, between representings and representeds. It explains the constitutive reciprocal relations between normative attitudes and normative statuses: how attitudes both institute norms and answer to them. And it explains the relations between those two stories: how *normative practices* bring about *semantic relations*—indeed, specifically representational semantic relations—between thought and reality. Hegel extends Rortyan (and Deweyan) pragmatism by explaining how what one is practically *doing* in recollecting (the *process* and *practice* of producing a retrospective recollective rational reconstruction of a course of experience as expressively progressive) provides the basis for an *expressive* semantic account of normative *representational relations* between the human and the nonhuman. Hegel understands what things are *in themselves*—objective reality—in terms of the functional role represented reality plays in our discursive practices as normatively governing our claims about it (in the double-barreled, deontic and alethic sense of "normative governance"). He appeals to the notion of *recollection* to specify the fine structure of the attitudes that acknowledge something as playing that role. How things are *in* themselves is seen to emerge recollectively from a sequence of how things show up *for* consciousness (the *reality* behind what are now visible as appearances *of it*).

This is the core of the *idealism* Hegel propounds in the *Phenomenology*: understanding the *concept* of *objective reality*, how things really are, how they are in themselves (*an sich*, implicitly), in terms of the functional role that assigning that status to some conception plays in the process of experience. Particularly important is the role that status plays in the recollective phase of experience, which is the phase in which how things really are (what was all along being represented) is uncovered, expressed with ever greater explicitness and fidelity, as governing a curated, cumulative, progressive sequence of its appearances (representings of it). Recollective reconstruction of an epistemic tradition culminating in and vindicating entitlement to the current constellation of commitments exhibits represented reality as at once the cause of sense and the goal of intellect. For recollection reveals the objective, represented reality as *governing* the expressively progressive appearances representing it in the dual sense that the representings are subjunctively sensitive to what they represent and that what they represent serves as a normative standard for assessments of the correctness of those representings. The key criterion of adequacy of *successful* recollection is that it rationally reconstruct a sequence of representing appearances culminating in veridical grasp of what was all along represented, in a way that satisfies those twin alethic modal and deontic normative demands. Hegel's idealism is not the wacky reference-dependence claim that apart from such recollective activities on the part of knowing subjects there would *be* no objective reality (which he derides under the rubric "subjective idealism"). It is the sense-dependence claim that we must *understand* what we *mean* by our talk and thought about objective reality in terms of the role it plays in the recollective production of *reasons* entitling us to our commitments concerning how things really are.[13] Rortyan pragmatists and Hegelian idealists agree that there is a way of understanding the notion of *reality* that comes as part of a package that includes the concept of *representation*. It is the conception Rorty marks with the snarky uppercase "R" in "Reality." His serious intent is to accept the concept of *reality* as playing *only* the role of cause of sense, rejecting the idea that it also should be understood as playing the normative role of goal of intellect. I have been arguing that Hegel's recollective idealism shows pragmatists how they can

---

[13] Here I am ruthlessly selectively summarizing just one strand in the more nuanced discussion of Hegel's idealism in *A Spirit of Trust*. There his absolute idealism is dissected into three concentric theses: bimodal hylomorphic conceptual realism, the reciprocal sense-dependence claim of objective idealism, and what I call "conceptual idealism." It is the third of these claims, centering on the recollective phase of the process of experience, that I sketch here.

embrace the full-blooded conception of reality without violating their well-taken scruples.

Both Rorty and Dewey avowedly and evidently learned important lessons from Hegel's historicism. Both distinguished themselves from their fellow philosophers by the extent to which they in fact practiced the recollective rationality that Hegel preached. Their different but largely consonant diagnoses of the ills of their respective philosophical milieus took the form of sweeping metaconceptual narratives of the intellectual heritage and traditions that shaped them. (This is what Rorty was talking about under the self-deprecatory rubric of "ambitious, swooshy, *Geistesgeschichte*" that I quoted early in the first lecture.) Yet from my point of view Rorty and Dewey both failed in the end to appreciate the overarching significance of Hegel's historicism. For they did not pay sufficient attention to the reconception of rationality at its core: Hegel's invention of the metaconcept of *recollective rationality* as the structure of *Vernunft*, and the philosophical work he called on it to do in understanding both the transitions to and beyond modernity and (so) in reconciling social pragmatism with what was right about representationalism.

I have argued that Hegel presents a detailed, constructive, anti-authoritarian, nonfetishistic, unalienated, social pragmatist account of the representational dimension of conceptual content. He thereby offers a concrete *pragmatist* alternative to global semantic and epistemological anti-representationalism. He anticipates the challenge to the very idea of objective reality as providing norms for thought that Rorty sees fundamental Enlightenment insights as mounting. This was the lesson Rorty thought required for us a second Enlightenment to appreciate. But Hegel sees Rortyan *irony* (no less than the Romantic irony from which it develops) as theoretical and practical *alienation* from the tradition-constituting and tradition-articulating norms—as ultimately a confession of failure to reconcile their acculturating role in making us what we are with our role in instituting those norms. This is the failure to bring together in one vision the two senses in which the norms are *ours*: the sense in which we make them and the sense in which they make us by acculturating us (*Bildung*). Already in 1806 he anticipated Rorty's argument, and the alienating, ironic, but authentically anti-authoritarian pragmatist challenge to the intelligibility of the representational paradigm that Rorty offers on behalf of our responsibility to reasons, and so to each other as reason-givers. Hegel's pragmatist account of the fine structure of normativity in terms of the way reason in its recollective function administers the interplay of attitude-governing normative statuses and norm-instituting attitudes shows how the emancipation from alien authority the Enlightenment promised can be achieved without the alienation that its insights seemed to entail.

I want to close by reverting to the "Kant oder Hegel?" question with which I began my first lecture. From the point of view of the Hegelian response I have rehearsed to the anti-authoritarian, global anti-representationalist argument Rorty announced in Girona, Rorty appears himself to remain mired in alienated Kantian analytic *Verstand*, unable to make the momentous step to Hegelian recollective *Vernunft*. To this extent and in this respect, Rorty shows up as unable fully to disentangle himself from the coils of Kantian thought from which he had been struggling to wrestle free since *Philosophy and the Mirror of Nature*, as he rigorously followed out what he saw as the consequences of the social pragmatism about normativity that he extracts from what Dewey made of Hegel. I take it that the analysis I have offered here leaves the discussion with a new, heightened and transformed, specifically *pragmatist* version of the "Kant oder Hegel" question. Should pragmatists embrace the concepts of *representation* and its associated understanding of the reality we represent, reconstrued along Hegelian lines of recollective rationality? Should the concept of *experience* be rehabilitated as Hegelian *Erfahrung*? To do so would be to complete the circle Rorty began when he rejected what he properly understood as ultimately Kantian conceptions of representation and experience in *Philosophy and the Mirror of Nature*. The question then becomes whether pragmatism's advance from Kant should be understood and developed in Rorty's way, or in Hegel's. I prefer to see Hegel's way of understanding the representational semantic dimension of discursive normativity as a friendly amendment: a development within the broadly pragmatist tradition Rorty champions. But Rorty might well be inclined rather to take it as evidence of just how hard it is even for philosophers with substantial pragmatist sympathies to free themselves from the Kantian legacy that has hindered us from completing the work of the Enlightenment.

AFTERWORD*

The material on which my Spinoza lectures at the University of Amsterdam in 2021 were based, presented here in slightly expanded form, is my most recent contribution to an extended conversation with Richard Rorty that has been going on now for many decades. While I was first writing these lectures, I was consulting with Eduardo Mendieta as he edited and prepared for the publication of Rorty's 1996 Ferrater Mora Lectures at the University of Girona.[1] In the Foreword to that volume, I recount the intense discussions I had there with Rorty, John McDowell, and Bjorn Ramberg. These lectures articulate a line of thought that I now, twenty-five years later, wish I had been in a position to contribute to those interactions. (*L'esprit d'escalier* on an extended time scale!)

The broad context of my long-standing conversation with Rorty was a shared understanding of twentieth-century philosophy as riven by two competing approaches to language. Rorty had organized his influential 1967 anthology *The Linguistic Turn*

---

* A literary device expressing recollective reflections on the origins of the work.
[1] Mendieta, *Pragmatism as Anti-Authoritarianism*.

around the opposition between "ideal language philosophy" and "ordinary language philosophy." The first is the tradition of Frege, Russell, the Wittgenstein of the *Tractatus*, Carnap, Tarski, and Quine, which in the hands of his Princeton colleagues Kripke and Lewis was flowering into possible worlds semantics. Inspired by Frege's idea of logic as a perspicuous artificial met-alanguage for expressing mathematical concepts, its goal is formal semantic calculi that can mathematically codify meanings. By the time he wrote *Philosophy and the Mirror of Nature*, Rorty had come to think of this twentieth-century movement as just the contemporary shape taken by the Enlightenment representationalism that was initiated by Descartes and brought to its canonical form by Kant.

By the 1970s I think Rorty had substantially—and usefully—broadened his conception of the contrasting way of thinking about language. Ordinary language philosophy now took its place as merely one manifestation of a larger current of thought. This is a broadly anthropological approach focused on the *use* of language, rather than on meanings. It understands language in the first instance as a distinctive kind of social practice, and thinks of engaging in such discursive practices as a striking feature of the natural history of a certain kind of organism. Where the logistical tradition takes as its paradigm the mono-logical derivation of consequences in a rigorous rule-governed proof system, the anthropological-sociological tradition takes as its paradigm dialogical interactions among biological creatures, subject to multifarious contingent and evolving norms. This more capacious conception of the rival to the representationalist semantic tradition encompasses the classical American pragmatists, the later Wittgenstein, and even the early Heidegger. It is this tradition, looking to use rather than meaning, practice rather than concept or content, recommending the pursuit of pragmatics (in a broad sense) rather than semantics, that Rorty would come to call "pragmatism," in the form it takes after the linguistic turn.

Rorty and I both oriented ourselves by something like this picture of the philosophical treatments of language we inherited, as either concerned with semantics to the exclusion of pragmatics (meaning rather than use) or concerned with pragmatics to the exclusion of semantics (use rather than meaning). We differed about the character of this bifurcation, and consequently about the lesson to be drawn from it as to what would count as a progressive step forward from the impasse we took to be its result. Rorty saw the two camps as motivated by incompatible visions and aims. The therapy he recommended given that diagnosis was to sharpen the distinction between them, so as to force a decision: a choice of one of these options. He accordingly argued for his distinctive way of developing pragmatism as a replacement for the wrongheaded representationalist tradition that he saw as a degenerating research program, doomed to collapse under its internal contradictions.

By contrast, I saw the logistical-semantic and anthropological-pragmatic approaches as ultimately complementary rather than competing, and as calling for a synthesis of them rather than a choice between them. As actually worked out, each was one-sided (in the sense Hegel gave to the term "*einseitig*"). Philosophers in the lineage that stretched from Frege to Lewis had not in fact thought much about the practices of using linguistic expressions so as to confer on them the meanings, including the representational significances, that they developed tools to characterize. But I saw no reason they could not do so. Quine himself was one of Rorty's pragmatist heroes precisely because of his criticisms of Carnap for, in effect, inappropriately assimilating natural languages, where meanings had to be instituted by the ground-level use of expressions, to artificial calculi, whose meanings were attached by stipulation in more expressively powerful semantic metalanguages. Yet he was also an avatar of extensional representational semantics. And Quine's student (and my teacher) David Lewis did worry about the use of language, in his book *Convention* (working up material from his Harvard dissertation), and especially in his classic essay "Languages and Language" and in his work on conversational scorekeeping (which I would draw on in *Making It Explicit*). Davidson (also a Quine student) is another one whom Rorty worked hard to recharacterize as a pragmatist ally. Yet he, too, had recursive truth-theories at the heart of his systematic enterprise. The *philosophical* semantics that studied the relations between pragmatics and semantics—how expressions must be used in order to have the meanings that *formal* semantics aims to specify with mathematical precision—might in fact be underdeveloped by the logistical tradition. But I saw no reason to think that the general approach somehow ruled out telling suitable pragmatic stories.

And the situation seemed comparable on the other side. It is true that Rorty's favorite classical American pragmatists, James and Dewey, were not much interested in logic, mathematics, or the sort of semantics Tarski and Carnap pursued. But, as Cheryl Misak has emphasized, there was also the lineage of pragmatists stretching from Peirce and C.I. Lewis to Sellars that did care about these issues, tools, and projects.

Wittgenstein does seem to have been on Rorty's side of things here, recoiling from his *Tractarian* representationalism to his *Investigations* pragmatism in terms that manifest his conviction that pursuing the one sort of project is incompatible with pursuing the other. One model of the relation between pragmatics and semantics understands meanings or conceptual contents (beginning with propositional contents) as standing to the norm-governed abilities or practices that are the use of linguistic expressions as theoretical objects stand to observable ones. The point of postulating semantic interpretants associated with utterances is then taken to be to codify systematically the practical proprieties that govern the use of the expressions uttered. When the later Wittgenstein is viewed through the lens of this theory/observation model (as Dummett recommends we do) two interpretive possibilities become visible. Some of Wittgenstein's formulations suggest that he is a semantic nihilist because he is in effect a behaviorist instrumentalist. On this reading, he does not think it is appropriate to use the method of postulating unobservable theoretical entities to understand implicitly normative discursive practices. (This could be one of the many strands of thought that come together in his dictum that "Philosophy is not one of the natural sciences.") One should stay at the pragmatic "surface" of proprieties of use, and not seek to delve "deeper" or look for something "behind" discursive behavior. (Dummett favors this reading, and at least started out by adopting a similar view himself.) This instrumentalist view is one of Sellars's particular targets in "Empiricism and the Philosophy of Mind." There he argues that there is no more reason to be ontologically chary about the existence of theoretical entities in the philosophy of mind (and, we can add, semantics) than there is in physics. The distinction between observables and theoretical posits is epistemological and methodological, not ontological. It is a difference in how we know things (by observation or exclusively by inference), not a difference in kind of thing known. And the line between those different kinds of accessibility can shift with time.

A more charitable interpretation takes Wittgenstein's semantic skepticism to be more broadly empirical. He thinks the plastic, protean character of discursive practice makes it impossible in practice to codify it theoretically in a general or systematic way. At most a semantic theory would allow one to offer a snapshot characterizing the current time-slice of a constantly and rapidly changing motley.[2] On either way of understanding him, it seems clear that the last thing the later Wittgenstein thinks philosophers should be doing is the kind of systematic transcendental theorizing about the necessary semantic (representational) structure of all possible languages that he provided the paradigm for in his *Tractatus*. Rorty stands in full solidarity with him on this point.

Like the later Wittgenstein, the early Heidegger rejects the traditional picture of the world as in the first instance explicitly represented ("merely present," the conception of *Vorhandensein*) in favor of a story that starts with the practical, implicit availability of things (as "equipment," the conception of *Zuhandensein*) in norm-governed practices, including discursive ones. Though Heidegger's views, like Wittgenstein's, display a substantial *Kehre* requiring us sharply to distinguish early views from later ones, his repudiation of what Rorty (in good company with others such as Dreyfus and Haugeland) thinks of as the pragmatism of *Being and Time* is emphatically *not* in the direction of what anyone in the semantic tradition would recognize as a contribution to their enterprise. On the contrary, what he later finds objectionable about this work, which he characterizes as juvenile and merely anthropological, is precisely the remnants of the views of his neo-Kantian teachers that might permit the recuperation, revival, or reconceptualization of that semantic strand of the Kantian legacy. After his turn, the social practical notions of *Mitsein* and *Zuhandenheit* fall away. It was still possible to read the early work as presenting not only a social pragmatics of

---

[2] I consider these alternatives further in "Some Strands of Wittgenstein's Normative Pragmatism, and Some Strains of His Semantic Nihilism," in *Disputatio: Philosophical Research Bulletin*, special issue: *Linguistic and Rational Pragmatism: The Philosophies of Wittgenstein and Brandom*, 2019.

discursive practice but also, on that basis, a unique approach to semantics, if, as I did, one centered one's interpretation on the principle that the meaning of "Being" is the being of meaning.[3] Perhaps the view lives on in the later slogan that "language is the house of Being" (which prompted Derrida's vision of philosophizing as dancing around the house of Being).

So in his expanded coterie of philosophical pragmatists Rorty could find some good company for understanding commitment to approaching the study of language through the social practices of using linguistic expressions as superseding or ruling out the sort of semantic concerns whose paradigm topic is specifically representational content. I was not persuaded that his pragmatist predecessors had better arguments for this exclusionary stance than Rorty himself did. In the first lecture here, I sketch my understanding of the way his position evolved, on its way to what seems to me the most cogent and promising development of it, in his Girona lectures. But my interest was always more in the constructive challenge both to do justice to pragmatics and to incorporate semantics than I was in the critical arguments against representational semantics in its various incarnations. I think that pragmatists should tell a semantic story. At the very least, the prospects for doing semantics in a pragmatist spirit should be more thoroughly explored than they have been. It seems to me that the pragmatist semantic project

---

[3] I elaborated views along these lines in the two essays on Division One of *Being and Time* reprinted in *Tales of the Mighty Dead*. I first ran across the phrase "the meaning of Being is the being of meaning," which I still regard as deeply insightful, as a playful and not at all respectful verbal example in Grover, Camp, and Belnap's classic essay "The Prosentential Theory of Truth," *Philosophical Studies: An International Journal for Philosophy in the Analytic Tradition*, Vol. 27, No. 2, February 1975, pp. 73–125, where it served as the anaphoric antecedent of the further remarks "That's profound," "And it's true."

that defines the lineage of Peirce, C.I. Lewis, Quine, Sellars, and Davidson remains worth pursuing.

I had the immense privilege and singular advantage of talking with Rorty about this issue, in depth and on innumerable occasions, for essentially the whole thirty-five years of our face-to-face association—from when I first sought him out upon my arrival at Princeton as a bright-eyed (but already furry-faced) new graduate student in 1972, until his death in 2007. Like Dewey, the early Heidegger, and the later Wittgenstein, he saw pragmatism as offering a new way forward that should disencumber itself from the weighty baggage of representational approaches to mind and language. Such approaches, he thought, were methodologically crippled by focusing on a model of meaning that worked reasonably well for sentences like "the frog is on the log," but would never help us understand any more interesting claims, like "freedom is better than slavery," or "the conceptual transformations wrought by the Newtonian paradigm shift were even more radical and far-reaching than those wrought by the later Einsteinian one." Rather than attempting to preserve the semantic tradition from Kant to Carnap, and synthesize it with the insights motivating pragmatism, his idea was that the representationalist way of thinking should simply be abandoned as of merely antiquarian interest, however much we might appreciate the effort and ingenuity it represented—according it the same status for contemporary thought as we now do to Plotinus's Neoplatonism, or Ockhamism—as he once put the point to me. That challenging view has always been an orienting landmark for my philosophical work, and the conversation that grew up around it is both longstanding and ongoing. These Spinoza lectures are just my latest contribution to it.

In my first lecture I sketched a retrospective rational reconstruction of the development of Rorty's anti-representationalist arguments, which structured his side of this conversation. It will be immediately clear to anyone who persists to the end of the story I tell in these lectures that it is itself an instance of the sort of recollective retrospective rational reconstruction of a tradition as expressively progressive that I describe in the second lecture. I stand by this story. But it is also clear to me in retrospect that that story is, in addition, an exercise in attempting to exhibit intellectual phylogeny as recapitulating my particular intellectual ontogeny. For I began my philosophical career challenged by Rorty's principled semantic skepticism—while being also motivated by a conviction that there the latest work in formal semantics not only expressed deep insights, but also represented substantial philosophical progress. And over the course of my career, I both became clearer about how Rorty's objections worked, and, eventually, about how they might be responded to. Many of the raw materials for the response, it seemed to me, I had learned from Hegel.

Assuming that one aspires to do justice both to semantics and to pragmatics, and to integrate those accounts, there are two paths one might pursue to achieve a synthesis or combination. One could take the representational semantics for granted and try to work out how one would need to use expressions to confer meanings of that sort on them. (That is what Lewis does in "Languages and Language.") We could call the order of explanation that starts with a notion of content that is explicated and motivated independently of its relation to acts, abilities, or practices *"semanticist."* Or one could take the social practical picture for granted, and try to work out what sort of content could be conferred on expressions by being suitably caught up in practices of that sort. This is the pragmatist order of explanation. The strategies I have experimented with started from the pragmatic side, and proceeded from there to the semantic side.

Here is an example of what I mean. Frege observes that asserting or judging is taking-true. That principle can be exploited in two directions. One can start with a story about truth, and then say what it is to take or treat something *as* true, to put it forward as true (as having that property). Or one could start with a story about asserting or judging and understand truth as what one is putting something forward as, the property one is taking a content to have by endorsing it in asserting or judging it. What I call "semantic pragmatism" is the claim that the point of postulating meanings or conceptual contents associated with linguistic expressions is to explain or codify (proprieties or implicit norms governing) their use. What I call "methodological pragmatism" is the claim that all there is to establish the association between linguistic expressions and semantic interpretants (contents, meanings, truth conditions, referents, extensions…) for expressions of natural ("ordinary") language is the use that is made of them. By contrast, for artificial ("ideal") languages, semantic interpretants are typically associated with linguistic expressions by stipulation, in an expressively more powerful explicit metalanguage. Semantic and methodological pragmatism are two ways of filling in the claim that "semantics answers to pragmatics." This is the sort of pragmatism I have been interested in exploring.

Rorty devotes one of his Girona lectures to addressing my systematic constructive semantic efforts in *Making It Explicit*, which had come out three years before. At the center of the account I offer there is the concept of *inference*. It guides the discussion both of pragmatics and of semantics. On the one hand, discursive practice is understood as having at its core practices of giving and asking for reasons, that is, practices of asserting and inferring. These two kinds of doings are seen as part of one practically indissoluble package. Assertions are what both can be given as reasons, that is, play the role of premises in inferences, and for which reasons can be given, that is, can play the role of conclusions of inferences. Asserting and inferring are things that are *done*, in a more full-blooded sense than merely representing is. They are normatively significant performances caught up in social practices of assessing their correctness. Because of their inferential practical significances, assertible (which is to say, propositional) contents stand to one another in relations of implication and incompatibility. Those reason relations are rich enough to permit the development of a recognizably *semantic* theory that need not at the outset appeal to a notion of *representation*.

In Section VI of the first lecture I sketch the sort of semantics I think Rorty could endorse. Like the semantic inferentialism I recommend, it looks to the role expressions play in practices of justification, of asking each other for reasons and giving reasons to each other, in order to understand the conceptual content expressed by those locutions. The difference between our positions is that he wanted to think of meaning (if at all), in terms of justification *rather than* truth. In contrast, I thought of identifying the role expressions play in reason relations as just the opening move in a justification-first order of explanation. The next stage in such an account would be to address the representational dimension of conceptual content: what leads us to distinguish what someone is talking or thinking *about* from what they are saying or thinking about it.

For an inferentialist semantics can support a subsequent account of the specifically representational dimension of conceptual content. In *Making It Explicit* that portion of the project appeals to the *social* character of discursive practice. The analysis is in two parts. We do commonly distinguish between what we are saying or thinking (a propositional content expressible using a declarative sentence or corresponding sentential clause) and what we are talking or thinking *of* or *about*, what is referred to or represented in that saying or thinking (expressible using a singular term or noun phrase). The claim that conceptual content has a representational dimension is accordingly not just a matter of high semantic theory. The locutions used to make explicit this representational dimension (quite apart from terms such as "refers" or "represents," which are technical theoretical terms) are *de re* ascriptions of propositional attitudes. These are sentences such as "Late in his life, Kant claimed *of* his loyal, hardworking servant that he was lazy and good for nothing." The idea is to understand the (implicit) representational dimension of assertible contents by looking at the expressive function of this sort of locution (what it makes explicit). The second phase of the argument is then an account of what we are *doing* when we assert such a *de re* ascription of propositional attitude. In making the ascription above, I am doing two things: *attributing* a claim to Kant and *undertaking* myself a further commitment to the effect that his servant Lampe, whom Kant took to be lazy and good for nothing, was actually (according to me) loyal and hardworking. The expressive function of the division in the ascription between terms applied within the scope of the "that" (the *de dicto* portion) and terms applied within the scope of the "of" (the *de re* portion) is to mark the distinction of social perspective between the commitments the speaker attributes and those the speaker undertakes herself.

The result is an account in a *pragmatic* metavocabulary that says what one is *doing* in *using* paradigmatically semantic representational vocabulary such as "of" or "about."[4] While the

---

[4] I tell this story in chapter 8 of *Making It Explicit*, and chapter 5 of *Articulating Reasons*.

cogency and adequacy of an account along these lines is of course open to challenge, it seemed to me to be a paradigm of the kind of explanation that Rortyan pragmatists ought to welcome. Some other philosophers friendly to Rorty's views (pragmatists after the linguistic turn) have endorsed cognate ways of carrying forward his project. Most notably, Huw Price, another anti-representationalist, linguistic-turn pragmatist, self-consciously downstream from Rorty, acknowledges the ordinary distinction between what we saying or thinking and are talking or thinking about, and applauds this sort of pragmatic analysis of it, by distinguishing between this harmless "internal-representational" notion and the objectionable "external-representational" ideas relied on by classical representationalist semantics.

In Girona, Rorty was not engaging with my systematic account at this level of detail. But he had a good sense of the general pragmatics-first broadly inferentialist semantic strategy that I was pursuing. A decade later, I devoted my John Locke lectures to developing a powerful and precise metavocabulary for perspicuously characterizing relations between the meaning and the use of linguistic expressions. This was the basis for what I called "analytic pragmatism." This sort of pragmatism was explicitly conceived as concerned with the relations between Rortyan vocabularies and the semantic and pragmatic metavocabularies used to talk about what we use those vocabularies to *say* and what we must *do* in order thereby to be using them to say those things. Only a few months before his death in 2007, Rorty heroically traveled to Prague to hear the version of those six lectures articulating that project that I gave there.[5] I pitched it as

---

[5] Those lectures were published the next year as *Between Saying and Doing: Towards an Analytic Pragmatism* (Oxford: Oxford University Press, 2008). A video of

offering a way of reconciling what was right about the semantic enterprise that was at the heart of analytic philosophy with the most basic insights motivating the pragmatist critiques of that enterprise that culminated in Rorty's own view. While graciously (as always) acknowledging my good pragmatist intentions, Rorty seconded—and literally applauded—the skepticism McDowell expressed there about my undertaking when he asked why I thought it worthwhile to try to transplant perfectly healthy pragmatist organs into the rotting corpse of analytic philosophy. Rorty simply could see no reason anyone who had understood the thrust of his critique should *want* to try to hold on to, or further develop, the Kantian semantic tradition of which analytic philosophy is evidently the most recent version. This view of his resonated sympathetically with McDowell's conviction that only someone who had completely missed the point of Wittgenstein's later work could respond to it by trying to craft a metalanguage expressively capable of systematically articulating something like all possible relations between the meaning and use of different vocabularies.

So before recruiting conceptual resources from Hegel to offer a pragmatist route to understanding the representational dimension of discursive practice, I had already put on the table a conception of pragmatism as a pragmatics-first approach to semantics, rather than a conception that saw pragmatics and semantics as exclusive alternatives, with pragmatics endorsed and semantics rejected. I had also suggested a social practical way of understanding at least one important representational dimension of discourse, recognition of which did not depend on

the Prague version of the lectures (originally delivered at Oxford in 2006), along with a video of Rorty's Girona lectures, as well as the original Spinoza lectures expanded here are available at https://www.youtube.com/c/BobBrandomPitt.

the flawed Kantian conceptions Rorty had diagnosed. What I add in the present lectures is the *historical* conception of rationality—recollective rationality—due to Hegel, that promises to complete the social conception of discursive practice and the reconception of the relations between pragmatics and semantics. Thinking about what Rorty might have made of it is one important way of continuing the extended conversation I have been talking about here.

REFERENCES

BOUVERESSE, JACQUES, "Reading Rorty: Pragmatism and Its Consequences," in Robert B. Brandom (eds), *Rorty and His Critics* (Oxford: Blackwell, 2000), pp. 129–145.

BRANDOM, ROBERT B., "A Hegelian Model of Legal Concept Determination: The Normative Fine Structure of the Judges' Chain Novel," in Graham Hubbs and Douglas Lind (eds), *Pragmatism, Law, and Language* (New York: Routledge, 2014), pp. 19–39.

BRANDOM, ROBERT B., *A Spirit of Trust: A Reading of Hegel's Phenomenology* (Cambridge, MA: Harvard University Press, 2019).

BRANDOM, ROBERT B., *Between Saying and Doing: Towards an Analytic Pragmatism* (Oxford: Oxford University Press, 2008).

BRANDOM, ROBERT B., "Expressive vs. Explanatory Deflationism about Truth," in Richard Schantz (ed.), *What Is Truth?* (Berlin: Hawthorne de Gruyter, 2002), pp. 103–119, reprinted in Bradley P. Armour-Garb and J.C. Beall (eds), *Deflationary Truth* (Chicago, IL: Open Court, 2005), pp. 237–257.

BRANDOM, ROBERT B., "Global Anti-Representationalism?," in Huw Price, Simon Blackburn, Robert Brandom, Paul Horwich, and Michael Williams, *Expressivism, Pragmatism, and Representationalism* (Cambridge: Cambridge University Press, 2013).

BRANDOM, ROBERT B., *Rorty and His Critics* (Oxford: Blackwell, 2000).

BRANDOM, ROBERT B., "Some Strands of Wittgenstein's Normative Pragmatism, and Some Strains of His Semantic Nihilism," in *Disputatio: Philosophical Research Bulletin*, special issue: *Linguistic and Rational Pragmatism: The Philosophies of Wittgenstein and Brandom*, 2019.

BRANDOM, ROBERT B., *Tales of the Mighty Dead* (Cambridge, MA: Harvard University Press, 2002).

BRANDOM, ROBERT B., "When Philosophy Paints Its Blue on Grey: Irony and the Pragmatist Enlightenment," *boundary* 2, Vol. 29, No. 2, Summer 2002, pp. 1–28.

ELIOT, T.S., *Four Quartets* (New York: Harcourt, Brace and Co., 1943).

GROVER, DOROTHY L., JOSEPH L. CAMP, JR., NUEL D. BELNAP, JR., "The Prosentential Theory of Truth," *Philosophical Studies: An International Journal for Philosophy in the Analytic Tradition*, Vol. 27, No. 2, February 1975, pp. 73–125.

GUPTA, ANIL, *Conscious Experience* (Cambridge, MA: Harvard University Press, 2019).

HEGEL, G.W.F., *Phenomenology of Spirit*, trans. A.V. Miller (Oxford: Oxford University Press, 1977).

HERDER, JOHANN GOTTFRIED, "Older Critical Forestlets," in Michael N. Forster (ed.), *Herder: Philosophical Writings* (Cambridge: Cambridge University Press, 2002), pp. 257–267.

LOCKE, JOHN, *An Essay Concerning Human Understanding* (Oxford, Clarendon 1959).

MATSON, WALLACE, "Why Isn't the Mind-Body Problem Ancient?," in P. Feyerabend and G. Maxwell (eds), *Mind, Matter, and Method* (Minneapolis, MN: University of Minnesota Press, 1966), pp. 92–102.

MENDIETA, EDUARDO (ed.), *Pragmatism as Anti-Authoritarianism* (Cambridge, MA: Harvard University Press, 2021).

MENDIETA, EDUARDO, *Take Care of Freedom and the Truth Will Take Care of Itself: Interviews with Richard Rorty* (Stanford, CA: Stanford University Press, 2005).

RORTY, RICHARD, *Contingency, Irony, and Solidarity* (Cambridge: Cambridge University Press, 1989).

RORTY, RICHARD, *El pragmatismo, una version: Antiautoristarismo en epistemologia y ética*, trans. Joan Verges Gifra (Barcelona: Ariel, 2000).

RORTY, RICHARD, "Incorrigibility as the Mark of the Mental," *The Journal of Philosophy*, Vol. LXVII, No. 12, 1970, pp. 399–424.

RORTY, RICHARD, "Intellectual Autobiography," in Randall E. Auxier and Lewis Edwin Hahn (eds), *The Philosophy of Richard Rorty* (Chicago, IL: Open Court Publishing, 2007).

RORTY, RICHARD, "Mind-Body Identity, Privacy, and Categories," *The Review of Metaphysics*, Vol. 19, No. 1, 1965, pp. 24–54.

RORTY, RICHARD, "Pragmatism as Anti-Authoritarianism," *Revue Internationale de Philosophie*, Vol. 53, No. 1, 207, 1999, pp. 7–20.

RORTY, RICHARD, "Pragmatism as Anti-Authoritarianism," in John R. Shook and Joseph Margolis (eds), *A Companion to Pragmatism* (Oxford: Blackwell, 2006), pp. 257–266.

RORTY, RICHARD, *The Linguistic Turn* (Chicago, IL: University of Chicago Press, 1967).

ROUSSEAU, JEAN-JACQUES, *The Social Contract and Other Later Political Writings*, trans. Victor Gourevitch (Cambridge: Cambridge University Press, 2018).

SELLARS, WILFRID, *Empiricism and the Philosophy of Mind* (Cambridge, MA: Harvard University Press, 1998).

WIERZBICKA, A., *English: Meaning and Culture* (Oxford: Oxford University Press, 2006).

WILLIAMS, MICHAEL, *Groundless Belief* (New Haven, CT: Yale University Press, 1977).

WITTGENSTEIN, LUDWIG, *Philosophical Investigations*, trans. G.E.M. Anscombe (New York: Macmillan, 1953).

INDEX